THE BUTTERFLY EMERGES

Finding Your Confidence in Christ

Dedicated to Landon
My first awesome grandchild

Based on the Original Caterpillar to Butterfly Workbook

Copyright © 2012 by Brenda Silveira

ISBN 978-0-9920271-3-1

Creator of I M CONFIDENT NIAGARA CANADA

Scripture verses are all taken from the King James Version of The Bible (public domain).

IMPORTANT - PLEASE READ BEFORE STARTING THIS WORKBOOK

THIS WORKBOOK IS FOR INFORMATION ONLY AND NOT INTENDED TO REPLACE ANY PROFESSIONAL HELP YOU ARE RECEIVING. USE IT IN CONJUNCTION WITH YOUR CURRENT SERVICES AND/OR PROGRAMS. IF YOU ARE FEELING OVERWHELMED BY LIFE SITUATIONS OR FEEL THIS WORKBOOK IS NOT HELPING YOU PROPERLY, PLEASE CONTACT YOUR HEALTH PROFESSIONAL FOR ASSISTANCE.

YOU ARE A VALUABLE GIFT FROM GOD! PLEASE TAKE CARE OF YOURSELF!

INTRODUCTION

Hello! I hope this workbook will inspire and motivate you to start on your own personal journey to find happiness and success. It doesn't matter how difficult your life has been up to this point or how discouraged you feel. If you are like many other people, you have probably searched endlessly for answers, but have found nothing that helps. Society pressures us to be the 'perfect person', but in our quest to become perfect we ultimately fail again and again. **It is impossible to be perfect in an imperfect world.** So let's work hard on becoming the best 'imperfect' person that we can be.

How can we find happiness and success? Is it even possible? **Yes**, if we have 2 **CRITICAL** factors - <u>confidence in our God-given abilities</u> and knowing that we are <u>esteemed by God</u>. Sadly many people struggle with their daily life not even aware of why they have difficulties. It took me almost to the age of 60 to realize why my life was in such turmoil. Then some life changing events caused me to stop speeding through life aimlessly and look deeply inside myself.

My personal journey started with extensive research on mental health issues and self-esteem. This was accomplished by reading books, searching the internet, listening to CD's, watching DVD's, talking with counselors and attending workshops. By increasing my knowledge base, I was able to do an **honest** self-evaluation, allowing me to see life from a different perspective.

My journey continued as I spent several months helping a local peer support group where I learned a lot of practical knowledge. This allowed me to help others, which in turn helped me grow emotionally and my confidence increased.

The next and most important part of my journey began when a special friend brought me to a local church where I instantly felt accepted by others and loved by God. I firmly believe that we all have an empty space in our lives that can only be filled with God's presence. My lack of confidence, low esteem and depression were caused by my lack of faith and believing that God was not there for me. Success and happiness are **NOT** possible if God is not the center of our lives. We are lost without Him. People try self-help methods to improve their mind or change their bodies and ignore working on building a closer relationship with God, then wonder why their life doesn't get better. Once God became the focus of my life, I was able to esteem myself through Him and everything changed. This doesn't mean I never have any more problems because we live in a broken world, but now I can face life with a positive perspective, knowing God is in control.

Happiness and success are possible, and you can have life of peace and joy, BUT - there are NO quick-fixes and NO easy methods as others may promise. However, if you can commit to a lifetime of hard work, patience and prayer, you will reap the rewards. God loves you and is there to help you. All you have to do is ask Him.

Good luck and God bless! Brenda Silveira, Creator of I M Confident

This workbook is based on the original Caterpillar to Butterfly Self-Esteem workbook. It contains information that has been gained through research, personal experience and Biblical references. The workbook is divided into 4 sections as follows:

SECTION ONE – A JOURNEY INTO SELF-AWARENESS

SECTION TWO – A JOURNEY INTO POSITIVITY

SECTION THREE – A JOURNEY INTO SELF-IMAGE

SECTION FOUR – SETTING GOALS

If you visit www.imconfident.com you can find links to 4 slide presentations that were created for the original Caterpillar to Butterfly Workbook, which does not include any references to the scripture verses found in this version of the workbook. If you would like a s**hort explanation of each verse, there is an alphabetical listing at the end of the workbook.**

This workbook will:
- ✓ help you find your hidden strengths and skills
- ✓ help you discover what 'blocks' are stopping you from making proper choices in life
- ✓ show you what stresses you have
- ✓ give you a list of your positive qualities
- ✓ help you change negative self-talk into positive self-talk
- ✓ help change unrealistic ideas about beauty
- ✓ help create a new self-image
- ✓ empower you to make life changes
- ✓ help you set realistic goals
- ✓ bring you closer to God

Success is possible if:
- • you have an open mind and heart
- • you read scripture and pray daily
- • you sincerely want to change your life
- • you commit to actively working on change
- • you don't give up
- • you continue daily on working towards your goals
- • you include (trusted) family and friends in your journey

YOU CAN HAVE A LIFE OF HAPPINESS AND SUCCESS IF YOU INCLUDE GOD IN YOUR JOURNEY. THE CHOICE IS YOURS. Making choices can be difficult and change is never easy. Many people choose to continue living with stress and anxiety because they fear what change could bring. In reality, the benefits that come from making positive changes will far outweigh any reason you would have for staying where you are right now.

Stop making excuses and let's get started on creating a new you! Say goodbye to fear and anxiety and say hello to confidence and strong esteem! God is waiting to help you!

Try not to rush through the workbook. There is a lot of information to read and absorb. Do a page or two at a time and think carefully about what you have read. Take time to do the exercises and review your answers. When you have completed the workbook, keep it handy so when you are feeling a little stressed or overwhelmed by life, you can go back and review what you have learned.

If you have any questions or comments, please send an email to brenda@imconfident.com. I am praying for your success!

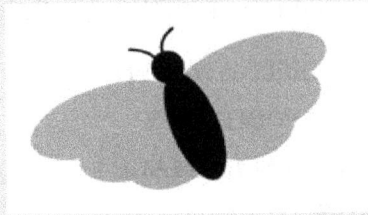

THE BUTTERFLY EMERGES!

A JOURNEY TO HAPPINESS & SUCCESS

OUR BODY
...is the hardware that makes us a person

OUR MIND
... is the part of us that thinks, feels, reasons, judges

OUR SOUL
...is the emotional and moral part of us that understands self & relates to others

OUR SPIRIT
... is the inner part of us that relates to God and discovers peace and joy

THE BUTTERFLY EMERGES
PART ONE
A Journey into Self-Awareness

> For we are his workmanship, created in Christ Jesus unto good works, which God hath before ordained that we should walk in them. Ephesians 2:10

DO YOU KNOW WHO YOU ARE?

Many people would have difficultly answering this question as they don't really know themselves very well. We live our lives according to what others expect and often lose our own unique identity.   We see flaws, imperfections, failures and are on a relentless mission to be like somebody else. We fail to see that we are a masterpiece created by God.

IN PART ONE, we will take you on a journey inside your mind and soul to help you understand the person you really are.   Self-awareness is the first step to finding happiness and success.   This first step will be one of many needed to build your confidence and increase your esteem.

Let's start by comparing your life to the life of a butterfly and ask these questions:

Are you a CATERPILLAR ......just crawling along the path of life, going nowhere in particular?

Maybe you are a PUPA (Cocoon)......hanging around, waiting for life to happen.

Or are you a BUTTERFLY......flying high and free, showing your beauty and confidence to all?

After completing this section, you should be able to understand yourself better and see life from a different perspective.

Do keep in mind that **success will require lots of your time and patience**. You **WILL** encounter difficulties and setbacks, but you **MUST** keep going even when you get discouraged or feel depressed.   As the saying goes, "Rome wasn't built in a day"; and change won't come as quickly as you want. People today want everything to happen instantly and this isn't possible. However, if you do build some good, positive habits, you will soon notice that positive changes are happening.   Talk to God daily and He will help you make those necessary changes.

BUTTERFLIES ARE BEAUTIFUL!

Take a look at some pictures, or even visit a butterfly garden to view the spectacular colours of their wings. How marvelous it would be to fly free, spreading your wings and showing your beauty to all!

Butterflies were once just plain ordinary caterpillars. How did something so plain become so beautiful? It's all in the plans of nature that guide the butterfly through 4 distinct stages where they grow and struggle to become transformed as a new creature.

STAGE 1 – THE EGG STAGE

STAGE 2 – THE CATERPILLAR OR LARVAE STAGE

STAGE 4 – THE BUTTERFLY OR ADULT STAGE

STAGE 3 – THE PUPAL OR CHRYSALIS STAGE

And be not conformed to this world: but be ye transformed by the renewing of your mind, that ye may prove what is that good, and acceptable, and perfect, will of God. Romans 12:2

BABIES ARE BEAUTIFUL!

People go through stages in life that are similar to the stages in a caterpillar's life. Let's take a look at how this unfolds.

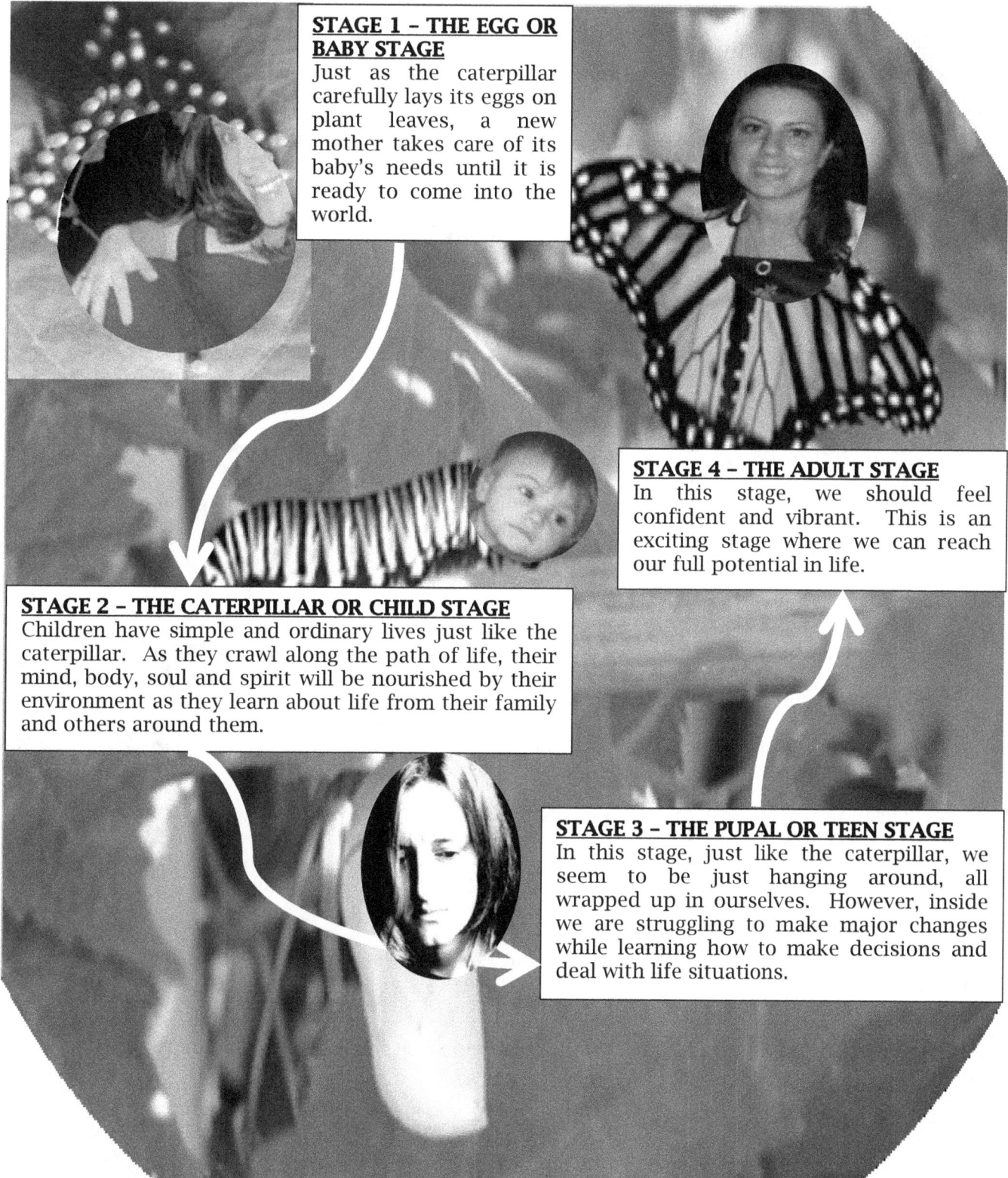

STAGE 1 – THE EGG OR BABY STAGE

Just as the caterpillar carefully lays its eggs on plant leaves, a new mother takes care of its baby's needs until it is ready to come into the world.

STAGE 4 – THE ADULT STAGE

In this stage, we should feel confident and vibrant. This is an exciting stage where we can reach our full potential in life.

STAGE 2 – THE CATERPILLAR OR CHILD STAGE

Children have simple and ordinary lives just like the caterpillar. As they crawl along the path of life, their mind, body, soul and spirit will be nourished by their environment as they learn about life from their family and others around them.

STAGE 3 – THE PUPAL OR TEEN STAGE

In this stage, just like the caterpillar, we seem to be just hanging around, all wrapped up in ourselves. However, inside we are struggling to make major changes while learning how to make decisions and deal with life situations.

IN A POSITIVE ENVIRONMENT

......our parents and peers give us and others, love and attention. They make us feel loved, wanted and appreciated. They provide us with a positive example of how we should live our lives.

We are given encouragement and see others around us treated with kindness and respect. We come to an understanding that God loves us and we can find our esteem through Him. This helps us grow with confidence and we develop a strong sense of personal worth.

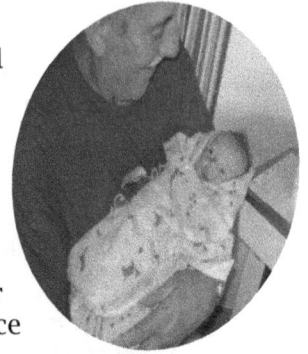

If we are fortunate to grow up in a mainly positive environment, we will be able to break free from our pupal or chrysalis stage and move forward with confidence. When life's difficulties come our way, we will be able to look at them from a positive perspective and deal with them effectively. We will also be able to set and work towards realistic goals.

When we understand how valuable we are, we can have the vibrant, exciting life of a butterfly for most of our lives. Stressful life situations will always jump in and cause temporary setbacks, but having confidence and strong esteem will help us bounce back quickly. We will also be empowered to move forward in life and reach our goals.

IN A NEGATIVE ENVIRONMENT...

......our parents and peers treat us and others badly. We may be in an abusive or neglectful situation and get little or no support. We see no positive examples of how to live our lives.

This causes us to feel unloved, unwanted and unappreciated. Our confidence does not grow and we believe that our lives have little or no value.

Living in a mainly negative environment creates fears and insecurities. We feel trapped in our pupal stage or we keep going back to the caterpillar stage. We can develop bitterness, anger and distrust which causes a lifetime of emotional distress.

Even if we are lacking in esteem, we might reach the butterfly stage for a short period of time. However, our lives will be full of struggles and problems. Stressful life situations will always cause setbacks. Having little confidence and little self-worth will keep the butterfly hidden from our lives and not allow us to make positive changes.

Many children grow up in an environment that is a positive/negative mixture which results in confusion and instability for the adult that emerges.

> **In a positive environment, we feel loved and appreciated which builds strong self-worth.**
> **In a negative environment, we feel unloved and unappreciated which destroys our self-worth.**

EACH OF US IS AT A DIFFERENT STAGE IN OUR LIVES.

WHAT STAGE ARE YOU AT?

CATERPILLAR?   **PUPA?**   **BUTTERFLY?**

Circle the stage you think you are at right now.

Why do you think you are at this stage? _____

_____

_____

What stage would you like to be at?   ☐ Caterpillar   ☐ Pupa   ☐ Butterfly

Why would you like to be at this stage? _____

_____

No matter what stage you are in right now, you don't have to stay there. You may feel like that lowly caterpillar crawling along the ground or like that future butterfly all wrapped up in itself, struggling to become confident, but there is good news. You are not born with esteem, it is something you learn, so you can develop it any age. Just remember that it takes time and patience to make positive changes in your life, but with strong faith and hard work you can become that beautiful butterfly!

I can do all things through Christ which strengtheneth me.   Philippians 4:13

HOW DO WE BECOME BUTTERFLIES?

This is accomplished by building confidence and discovering how valuable we are.

We can do this by:
1) Doing an honest self-evaluation
2) Learning self-acceptance
3) Improving our self-image, both inside and outside

1) SELF-EVALUATION

First we must do an honest self-evaluation by taking a close look at ourselves and trying to understand the person that we live inside. The problem is, most of us have distorted ideas about who we are because of things people have said to us in the past or because of the way people have treated us. This creates false beliefs that cause us to spend our lives trying to be like somebody else instead of being happy with who we are.

We need to discover our unique abilities, personality traits and expectations so we can find the real person inside – the unique individual that God has created. This will help us focus on our positive points and allow us to determine what changes need to be made so we can move forward in life.

YOUR SELF-EVALUATION

Read the following statements and circle the ones you believe about yourself.

1) I feel confident when talking to others.
2) I work hard and do a good job.
3) I know what my positive qualities are.
4) I try to keep my mind and body active.
5) I am a happy, carefree person.
6) I enjoy helping others.
7) I deserve love and respect.
8) I expect to have a good life.
9) I have set goals and work hard to achieve them.
10) I don't always believe what other people say about me.

How many did you circle? _____

These can be difficult statements to believe about yourself if you were raised in a negative environment and have low esteem, but YOU SHOULD BELIEVE EACH ONE OF THEM. Work on building your esteem, then revisit this checklist every few weeks and see if anything has changed.

On the next page there are some POSITIVE STATEMENTS or AFFIRMATIONS that you can use to start building some positive habits. Choose the affirmations that suit you best and start repeating them several times each day until you begin to believe them.

> I will praise thee; for I am fearfully and wonderfully made: marvellous are thy works; and that my soul knoweth right well.
> Psalm 139:14

POSITIVE AFFIRMATIONS

How often do you give yourself a compliment? Most people would never think of doing such a silly thing. But it isn't silly at all and we should all do this every day. Why? Because we are all special in our own way and we should always treat ourselves with kindness and respect.

Positive affirmations can "re-wire" your brain and give you a feeling of happiness, the power that can help you deal with the challenges you face each and every day.

When you get up in the morning, give your esteem a kick-start with a positive affirmation. Morning is the time when you are more likely to be relaxed and by initiating positive feelings first thing, it may stop you from worrying about the day ahead of you. **Repeat the affirmation often during the day until it fills up your brain with positive, encouraging power.** You will feel the difference in your attitude and this will reflect in your actions.

By continuing to use positive thoughts you will accomplish a lot. If you decide to continue with negative thoughts, you will likely accomplish little or nothing. Make sure that you ask God to help you develop these positive thoughts.

Change to a new affirmation daily or keep using a favourite one. One thing that is really important....DON'T just repeat your affirmations from memory and not pay attention to what you are saying because it won't work. If you really want to change your thinking, you have to listen to your words and say them with feeling. Here are a few suggestions:

· GOD LOVES ME UNCONDITIONALLY
· I HAVE A BEAUTIFUL SMILE
· I CAN MAKE A DIFFERENCE TODAY
· I WILL OVERCOME EVIL WITH GOOD
· I HAVE A WONDERFUL FAMILY
· I AM RELAXED AND PEACEFUL
· I FEEL GREAT
· I AM A TERRIFIC COOK
· I ALWAYS TRY MY BEST
· I HAVE A GREAT PERSONALITY
· I TREAT PEOPLE THE WAY I WANT TO BE TREATED
· I LOVE MYSELF BECAUSE GOD LOVED ME FIRST
· IT'S GOING TO BE A GREAT DAY
· I AM THANKFUL THAT I HAVE A JOB
· I ENJOY HELPING OTHER PEOPLE
· I AM A SPECIAL GIFT FROM GOD

CAN YOU THINK OF SOME MORE? Write them in the space below.

Me, Myself and I

The following is an exercise in self-awareness. In order to increase your esteem, you must become confident in who you really are. So let's find out some interesting things about you. Make sure you stay positive about yourself! Try doing this with a friend and share your answers.

🕐 My favourite time of day is _____ ♦ My favourite colour is _____

🏠 My favourite room in my house is _____ Why? _____

_____

🍽 My favourite food is _____

👤 My happiest memory is _____

👫 My friends like me because _____

🗣 The person who has influenced my life the most is (can be family, friend, public figure)

_____ Why? _____

_____

☺ My three best qualities are 1) _____

2) _____ 3) _____

🏅 My most difficult accomplishments are _____

_____

☝ The accomplishment I am most proud of is _____

🏆 My ultimate goal in life is to _____

☺ I wish _____

❶ If I could only use 1 word to describe myself, it would be_____

📖 How do you think God describes you? _____

> **Behold, what manner of love the Father hath bestowed upon us, that we should be called the sons of God: therefore the world knoweth us not, because it knew him not. 1 John 3:1**

2) SELF-ACCEPTANCE

This is a realistic awareness of our strengths and weaknesses. It is the ability to accept and not be critical of our imperfections, realizing that we all have unique worth and value. Good mental health requires us to accept ourselves and allows us to make effective life changes.

ACCEPTING YOURSELF

Read the following statements and circle the ones that are true.

1) I am a unique and valuable person.
2) I accept myself as I am and am happy with who I am.
3) I can accept criticism from others without feeling bad.
4) I admit that I make mistakes and do so openly.
5) I don't need approval from others to feel good.
6) I don't feel guilty when I say or do something I feel is right.
7) If I do something wrong, I try to make amends.
8) I am willing to try new things.
9) I believe that change can be good.
10) I know that I am God's child and I like who I am.

How many did you circle? _____

Accepting who you are is very hard to do. We often have an unrealistic view of ourselves because the world has set high expectations that we can never reach. This creates anxiety and depression for many people.

We have to become aware of our strengths and weaknesses and understand that it is impossible to be strong in all areas. We **DO NOT** have to be the 'super' person that does everything. By uncovering our strengths and weaknesses and accepting our imperfections and flaws, it will open the doors to a personal understanding of ourselves and lead the way to strong esteem. God has created us to be different than anyone else in the world and He loves us just the way we are. By listening to Him instead of listening to the world, we will realize our true value. If God loves and accepts us, then why can't we do the same thing?

WHAT ARE YOUR STRENGTHS AND WEAKNESSES? In the spaces below, list 5 of your strengths and 5 of your weaknesses. Did you know that many people find it easy to list their weaknesses, but have trouble listing their strengths? We focus on our weaknesses and feel bad about ourselves when we should be focusing on our strengths and trying to be the best person we can be. If you have any trouble finding your strengths, ask others to help. Sometimes other people see the best in us when all we can see is the worst.

STRENGTHS	WEAKNESSES
_____	_____
_____	_____
_____	_____
_____	_____
_____	_____

MY STRENGTHS

I feel my biggest strength is _____

This has helped me accomplish many things throughout my life such as _____

_____

_____

At this point in my life, I think others will remember me for _____

_____

MY WEAKNESSES

I believe that if I could have the following skills or characteristics, I would be more successful
and happy. _____

_____

_____

I wish I had handled the following situations differently in my life. _____

_____

_____

_____

If I could change one thing about myself, it would be _____

_____

_____

MY GOALS

I am going to improve myself with the help of (God, family, friends, taking a course, self-help)
by doing _____

_____

I feel that I am not using the following strengths to my full potential and am going to build on
these. _____

_____

The first thing I am going to work on changing is _____

_____

_____

I will build new strengths because I want others to remember me for _____

_____

_____

3) SELF-IMAGE

We show others how we feel about ourselves through our appearance and actions. First impressions are important when it comes to relationships and work, so we need to be careful about the image that we are presenting for others to see.

Being confident in our abilities and having strong esteem will help give us a positive self-image. These positive feelings come from knowing that God loves us and that He gives us strength. Our inner feelings of confidence help us develop a beautiful self-image from the inside out.

> But we all, with open face beholding as in a glass the glory of the Lord, are changed into the same image from glory to glory, even as by the Spirit of the Lord. 2 Corinthians 3:18

YOUR SELF-IMAGE

Read the following statements and circle the ones that are true.

1) I look good and I feel good.
2) I know what styles suit me and I dress to look good.
3) I feel confident in the clothing I wear and how I look.
4) I feel beautiful/handsome.
5) I know that others see me as a confident person.
6) I smile a lot because I feel good about myself.
7) I am not a perfect '10' and I know this isn't possible, but I feel perfect in God's eyes.
8) I don't look at other people to see how I should dress.
9) I am able to speak in public without fearing how I look.
10) I walk and talk with confidence.

How many did you circle? _____

Feeling good about your outward appearance is difficult.

Society puts a lot of pressure on us to be the 'perfect' person through images we see on television and in magazines. We see beautiful people living perfect lives, however these images are unreal and only created to sell products and services. Models and actresses work long hours to create these perfect images so companies can make a lot of money. But no matter how hard we try or how much money we spend, we will never be able to look perfect in an imperfect world.

Watching TV and reading magazines should be fun, not make us feel bad. This is why it is so important to feel good about our self-image and have strong esteem. We need to understand that looking good is not just about our outer appearance, it is also how we look on the inside which includes our character, God-given abilities and personal interests. When we have inner beauty, it will shine right through to the outside and people will notice our confidence.

Ask your family and friends how they feel about your appearance and what changes might help improve the way you look. Don't be afraid to try something new. Changing the way you look can influence your behaviour, build confidence and create a more positive attitude towards life. Keep one thing in mind – it doesn't have to cost a lot to create a new look - look for sales or check out bargain shops and second hand stores. Never go into debt to impress other people.

It is better to trust in the Lord than to put confidence in man. Psalm 188:8

BECOMING CONFIDENT IS HARD IN TODAY'S WORLD...

Society tells us:
*We are never good enough
*We lack something in our life
*We need to improve ourselves
*We need to be busier and quicker
*We need to have money/ possessions in order to be happy/successful

THIS IS NOT TRUE AND JUST LEADS TO STRESS! STRESS HAS BECOME AN ACCEPTED WAY OF LIFE, BUT THIS IS NOT ACCEPTABLE.

One major stressor that we have is comparing our lives to others who seem to have everything – beauty, possessions, money, lots of friends, great jobs, power, and so on. What we don't realize is that many of these 'lucky' people are not happy and they are also comparing themselves to others who have more than they do. The sad fact is, many of these 'lucky' people do not get what they really want and need – **LOVE**. Most of their so-called friends are only with them for personal gain and don't really care about the person at all.

Very few people are satisfied with what they have. Instead of wishing we had someone else's life, we should look at people who have less than we do and realize how much we really do have to be thankful for. God has given us so much!! Taking the focus off our wants and putting it on our needs would ultimately bring contentment and lessen stress.

We accept stress as normal and it certainly is, but not at the extreme levels that are happening today. By trying to become the **perfect** person in an **imperfect** world, we are just setting ourselves up for frustration and failure!! The following quiz will help you identify your stressors.

I get really stressed at work (school) when _____

_____

I get really stressed at home when _____

_____

The other times I get really stressed are _____

_____

The things that tell me I am really stressed are (e.g. headache, tight muscles, irritability, etc.)

_____

What I can do when I am really stressed _____

_____

But be not thou far from me, O LORD: O my strength, haste thee to help me.
Psalm 22:19

IT'S TIME TO STOP BEATING OURSELVES UP!

*Life is NOT perfect
*People are NOT perfect
*The grass is NOT really greener on the other side of the fence
*Happiness does NOT come from outside, it comes from inside each of us

SO WHAT CAN WE DO?
> Learn to love God and love others as we love ourselves

And thou shalt love the Lord thy God with all thy heart, and with all thy soul, and with all thy mind, and with all thy strength: this is the first commandment. And the second is like, namely this, Thou shalt love thy neighbour as thyself. There is none other commandment greater than these.
Mark 12:30,31

God created an AMAZING YOU, so start believing in yourself!

> You are the only one who can get yourself out of bed in the morning
> You are the only one who can plan your day
> You are the only one who can make your decisions, right or wrong
> You are the only one who can set your goals and values
> You are the only one who can determine what direction to take in your life
> You are the only one who can decide where you are going
> You are the only one who can change negative habits into positive habits
> You are the only one who can make you happy
> You are the only one who can change your life

Are you trying to change someone else? You CAN'T change another person, so stop trying. Only God can change people but you should pray and ask for His help. With God's help you CAN make positive changes in your own life and He will also work to make changes in the lives of the people around you.

Ask God to help you develop a more positive perspective on life so you can become a good example to others and influence them in a positive way. Prayer can be a very powerful change-making tool.

A positive attitude can affect the people around you in a positive way.

A negative attitude can affect the people around you in a negative way.

Would you rather be around positive or negative people? What kind of attitude do you have? HOW ARE YOU AFFECTING OTHERS?

How do we keep stress from becoming a serious problem?

Stress is a normal part of life and it affects our daily lives. It is a reaction to a person, thing or event and it can either motivate you to do something positive or something negative.

When stress motivates you to do something positive, it can energize you and move you forward in life. It can improve your mind, body, soul and spirit, giving you joy and peace. However, when stress motivates you to do something negative, it can cause physical and emotional problems. Research has proven this fact time and time again. Negative stress can literally suck the energy out of you, leaving you exhausted and depressed.

Research shows that many diseases are caused by stress including: headaches, indigestion, breathing problems, hypertension, sleeping disorders, heart disease, skin conditions and irritable bowel syndrome.

Following is a list of high stress situations that can happen in life. Circle the situations that have happened to you in the last 12 months.

1) Serious personal illness
2) Serious illness of someone close to you
3) Divorce or separation
4) Death of someone close to you
5) Move
6) Marriage
7) Pregnancy or birth of a child
8) Serious issues with children or someone close to you
9) Children leaving home
10) Job change, job loss or work problems
11) Retirement
12) Sleeping problems
13) Purchase of home or car
14) Serious financial problems or bankruptcy

> Stress is a normal part of life and it affects our daily lives.
>
> It can motivate you to do something positive or something negative.
>
> The choice is yours.

If you have checked off any of the first 4 situations, or more than 8 in the list, you are likely experiencing high levels of stress and should contact your family doctor for assistance.

If you have checked off 5 to 8 (not including a death or serious illness), you are experiencing more than the average amount of stress and should try to relax as much as possible.

If you have check off 3 or less (not including a death or serious illness), you are experiencing an average amount of stress.

However, each situation will cause different levels of stress for each individual and if you are feeling high levels of stress even for **just one** situation, you should try to find professional help.

Life is full of stressful situations that can affect your physical, mental and emotional health. If you find yourself in a situation that exhausts and overwhelms you, it is important to address the situation before it becomes a serious health matter. As the expression goes, "it is better to be safe than sorry".

Taking care of yourself is an important job that you can handle with the help of God.

CONTROLLING STRESS

Since it isn't possible to eliminate stress from life, it is important that we learn how to control it. Stress can actually give you positive energy, which can benefit you on your journey to becoming more confident. It is important to determine what causes the stress in your life and learn ways to minimize or eliminate it.

When you are stressed, try the following **STRESS** method:

Stop what you are doing.

Take note of the situation in your journal or notebook. Outline what is causing stress in your life.

Review your notes. Do this later in the day when you can sit down quietly by yourself. If you are too emotional, you won't see the situation clearly.

Evaluate your reaction. Was it proper, logical, realistic? Or did you blow the situation way out of proportion? Write down your answer.

Situation - can it be changed, minimized or eliminated? Yes? No? How? Write down your answer.

Set up a plan of action for the next time this situation come up. Write it down so you will remember it.

> Meditation is a great way to release stress. There are about 20 verses in The Bible that tell us we should meditate daily. Take some time each day to sit or lie down in a quiet place by yourself. Listen to some calming music. Breathe deeply. Close your eyes and allow the stress to leave your body. Starting from your head, relax each part of your body until you reach your toes.

Every day, write down your stressful situations in your journal or notebook. Use the above **STRESS** method as a guideline. Make sure you review the situation and make a plan of action.

What situation causes the most stress in your life? _____

_____

How do you react in this situation? _____

_____

Is it possible to change, minimize or eliminate this situation? ☐ Yes ☐ No How? _____

_____

Could you change your reaction to the situation? ☐ Yes ☐ No How? _____

_____

> **This book of the law shall not depart out of thy mouth; but thou shalt meditate therein day and night. Joshua 1:8**

NOW LET'S FIND THE BEAUTIFUL BUTTERFLIES

Go to where there is a mirror in your home and look closely at the person in the mirror. Who do you see?

NEWSFLASH!

The person you are looking at is the **ONLY** person in the world who can make you truly happy. **YES, IT'S TRUE!** Too many people believe that someone or something else will make them happy. They think that they will be happy when they finish school, get a job, get married or have children. They think that they will be happy when they get a big house, a new car or take that dream vacation. WRONG! External things will only bring happiness for a short period of time and then you will feel empty again.

If you want real, lasting happiness or joy, it comes from within and depends on your confidence and esteem. If you are connected to God, He will help you build your esteem and you will start to see life from a positive perspective. God will provide you with everything you need to live a life full of joy and peace.

Now, look in the mirror again and in the space below, write a short paragraph, as if you were describing yourself to another person. **ONLY WRITE POSITIVE COMMENTS! Don't include any unkind comments** that you have heard from others or that you tell yourself, as they are likely not true. Think about how God would describe you to another person.

When you are done, read your description out loud to yourself while looking in the mirror and make sure that you have been totally honest with yourself. If you have written anything negative, erase these comments and replace them with something positive.

I see myself as.........

Do this same exercise whenever you have negative thoughts about yourself. Replace any negative words with positive words and say them out loud over and over for reinforcement until you believe them.

YOU......ARE THE BEAUTIFUL BUTTERFLY!

✓**You don't have to let the world stress you out**

✓**You don't have to be like anyone else**

✓**You are one of a kind**

✓**You are unique**

✓**You are special**

✓**You are God's masterpiece!**

EVERY DAY LOOK AT YOURSELF IN THE MIRROR and REPEAT SEVERAL TIMES
"I am God's masterpiece and I am special".

THE MIRROR EXERCISE

Do your daily affirmations in front of a mirror. Hearing your own positive self-talk will have a powerful effect on you.

Get some paper and a pen, then complete the following statements as quickly as possible. Don't stop to think about the answer. When you are done, review your answers and change any that you haven't answered honestly.

This can also be done as group activity. *Sit in a circle and give everyone a list. The leader starts by choosing one of the following statements, then throwing a soft ball (or other object) to another participant who will finish the statement. This continues until all the statements have been used. More can be added and some can be duplicated if necessary.*

1) I am happiest when...
2) Right now, I'm feeling...
3) I like to be complimented on my...
4) I believe in...
5) This exercise makes me feel...
6) I am most ashamed of...
7) When I feel affectionate, I...
8) When I am alone, I...
9) A controlling person makes me feel...
10) I feel like I belong when...
11) When someone rejects me, I...
12) When I meet people for the first time, I...
13) My weakest (or strongest) point is...
14) The emotion I find hardest to control is ...
15) I am afraid of...
16) I like to be a follower (or leader) when...

For God so loved the world, that He gave His only son, that whoever believes in Him should not perish but have eternal life.   John 3:16

WHAT DO YOU LIKE ABOUT YOURSELF?

If the word 'nothing' comes to mind, you are not looking very hard. God has given each of us wonderful qualities. Everyone has some things they should like about themselves. You just need practice thinking positively. Here are some examples.

| I am fair to my employees. | I am a good cook. | I listen with a caring heart. | I am a great mom. | I like to take care of dogs. |

Now think about some things that you like about yourself and write at least 5 of them in the space below. If you have any trouble, ask your family and friends to give you some ideas.

HERE IS WHAT I LIKE ABOUT MYSELF

At the back of this workbook there is a page with 4 shapes called Positive Shapes. Cut out the shapes, than pick 4 things that you wrote in the space above and write 1 on each shape. Colour the shapes and decorate them any way you like and put them on your fridge, cupboard door or a mirror. Then each time you see the shape, read it out loud, with FEELING!

ALWAYS TRY TO BE POSITIVE

- Being positive doesn't come naturally.
- Good, positive habits need to be developed and any bad, negative habits need to be eliminated
- Creating good habits takes a lot of work and patience. A conscious effort on a daily basis is required.
- Daily prayer and scripture reading will help you develop good habits.
- When good habits are developed, they will likely rub off on other people.
- Being positive helps build confidence

DO SOMETHING POSITIVE
- Watch positive, uplifting programs on TV
- Listen to happy, upbeat music
- Read books that help you learn and grow
- Study scripture
- Make a list of your positive changes
- Start exercising regularly
- Meditate and pray daily
- Learn and practice proper breathing exercises
- Eat healthy foods
- Start or renew a hobby
- Join an interest group
- Visit a local church
- Laugh lots

SURROUND YOURSELF WITH POSITIVE PEOPLE
- Increase time spent with positive people
- Decrease or eliminate time spend with negative people (this may be difficult when you have negative family or close friends, but do your best)
- When around negative people, try to focus on being positive as it will help you and may influence them
- Get together with some friends and watch a funny movie or do some fun activities
- Get actively involved in a local church Bible study group and participate in their discussions and activities

TRY TO BE POSITIVE TOWARDS OTHERS
- Use kind, encouraging words
- Spend quality time with people you care about
- Give special gifts (simple & inexpensive)
- Volunteer for a local organization
- Be a positive example towards people who seem to be struggling
- Do acts of kindness in your community

BEING POSITIVE HELPS ALL OF US STAY HEALTHY

PHYSICALLY   EMOTIONALLY   SPIRITUALLY   MENTALLY

BELOW IS A LIST OF POSITIVE QUALITIES. CIRCLE THE ONES THAT DESCRIBE YOU

ABLE	CURIOUS	IDEALISTIC	PEACEFUL
ACCEPTING	DEPENDABLE	IMAGINATIVE	PERSISTENT
ACCURATE	DETERMINED	INDEPENDENT	PLEASANT
ADAPTABLE	DEVOTED	INDIVIDUALISTIC	POLITE
ADVENTUROUS	DYNAMIC	INDUSTRIOUS	PRACTICAL
AFFECTIONATE	EAGER	INFORMAL	PUNCTUAL
ALERT	EASY GOING	INGENIOUS	QUIET
AMBITIOUS	EFFICIENT	INTELLIGENT	RATIONAL
ARTISTIC	EMPATHETIC	INVENTIVE	REALISTIC
ASSERTIVE	ENERGETIC	JOYFUL	REASONABLE
ATTRACTIVE	ENTERPRISING	KIND	RELAXED
BENEVOLENT	ENTHUSIASTIC	LEARNING	RELIABLE
BOLD	FAIR-MINDED	LEISURELY	RESPONSIBLE
BROAD-MINDED	FAITHFUL	LIGHT-HEARTED	SELF-CONTROLLED
CALM	FIT	LIKEABLE	SENSIBLE
CANDID	FLEXIBLE	LOGICAL	SINCERE
CAPABLE	FORGIVING	LOVEABLE	SOCIABLE
CAREFUL	FREE	LOVING	SPECIAL
CARING	FRIENDLY	MATURE	STABLE
CAUTIOUS	FULFILLED	METHODICAL	STRONG
CHARMING	FUNNY	METICULOUS	SYMPATHETIC
CHEERFUL	GENEROUS	MILD	TACTFUL
CHILDLIKE	GENTLE	MODERATE	TALENTED
CLEAR-THINKING	GLAD	MODEST	THANKFUL
CLEVER	GOOD-NATURED	NATURAL	THOROUGH
COMPASSIONATE	GROWING	NEAT	TOLERANT
COMPETENT	HAPPY	NON-JUDGMENTAL	TRUSTING
CONFIDENT	HARD-WORKING	NURTURING	TRUSTWORTHY
CONSCIENTIOUS	HEALTHY	OPEN-MINDED	UNDERSTANDING
CONSIDERATE	HELPFUL	OPTIMISTIC	UNIQUE
CONTENT	HONEST	ORGANIZED	WARM
COOPERATIVE	HOPEFUL	ORIGINAL	WILLING
COURAGEOUS	HUMANE	OUTGOING	WITTY
CREATIVE	HUMOUROUS	PATIENT	ZANY

WE CAN ALL BE BUTTERFLIES!

Wouldn't this be a beautiful world if we were all butterflies!

Draw or paste your picture in the space below.

So God created man in His own image, in the image of God created He him; male and female created He them.   Genesis 1:27

THE BUTTERFLY EMERGES
PART TWO
A Journey into Positivity

What is planted in your garden of life?

We live in a garden that is called life. Your own personal garden was planted the day you were born and as you grew, your parents and other people around you started planting positive and negative seeds in your garden which has shaped you into the person you are today.

If positive seeds were planted, you will look at life with a positive perspective and have strong esteem. This will produce crops of beautiful words, kind thoughts and caring actions which will develop into Plants of Confidence, Bushes of Esteem, Flowers of Happiness and Trees of Success.

If negative seeds were planted, you will look at life with a negative perspective and have poor esteem. This will produce crops of mean words, unkind thoughts and cruel actions which will develop into Plants of Instability, Bushes of Insecurity, Flowers of Fear and Trees of Failure.

We need to plant our gardens carefully in order to establish roots firmly in the soil and help our lives become grounded in love. Then we need to provide continuous care to keep any nasty weeds from coming into our gardens and wiping away all the beauty.

Taking proper care of our garden of life will help us achieve our goals and give us the ability to influence our families, friends and the world around us.

PART TWO will take you on a journey through your garden of life where you will develop the skills needed to become more positive. It will help you learn how to change negative thoughts into positive thoughts and show you how to fill your inner self with positive energy.

> And the LORD God planted a garden eastward in Eden; and there
> he put the man whom he had formed. Genesis 2:8

A garden needs proper nourishment and care in order to grow. Certain things are necessary:

- Good seeds
- Fertile soil
- Watering
- Weeding
- Pruning
- Continuous care

When all these conditions are met, the garden will flourish. Plants will grow. Flowers will bloom. Trees will bear fruit. The garden will be full of life and beauty.

When butterflies lay their eggs, they know how important it is to choose the proper plant leaf so when the egg hatches, the baby caterpillar will have the proper nourishment. Just like the butterfly, we have to be careful that we give our children the proper nourishment so they will have the opportunity to develop strong esteem and grow into a responsible adult.

ALL LIVING THINGS NEED PROPER NOURISHMENT IN ORDER TO SURVIVE AND GROW.

Babies are nourished in their mother's womb where it is:

- Comfortable
- Warm
- Safe & secure

The mother needs to care for her own health while the baby is developing so it has the best possible conditions for proper growth. She should:

- Eat nourishing foods
- Exercise according to her health condition
- Get adequate sleep

The mother should also try to eliminate the use of harmful products such as:

- Alcohol
- Drugs
- Cigarettes

Ideally, the baby should be raised in calm, relaxing surroundings and it is the responsibility of the parents to do everything in their power to make this possible for their special, new baby.

Parenting is a huge responsibility and a lifetime commitment. The biggest influence on a child's development is the environment in which they grow up in. A positive environment is critical for building confidence and strong esteem, both of which are a prerequisite to success and happiness. A negative environment will stop a child from developing properly and can destroy any possibility of a good future.

Mistakes will undoubtedly be made since we are human. Life will always bring negative people and situations into our lives, but we need to try as hard as we can to be positive for our children and everyone around us.

THE SEED IS PLANTED IN FERTILE SOIL

A good gardener knows how important it is to plant 'good' seeds in fertile soil. Before planting anything, the soil needs to be nourished with fertilizer or compost and sometimes it is necessary to change to a new location so the nutrients aren't all depleted from the soil. When these conditions are met and the garden is cared for lovingly and consistently, the result will be healthy plants, flowers and trees.

It is just as important for parents to prepare the environment in which the child is to be born. A healthy child needs to grow up in a positive, loving environment surrounded by people who support them and help build their esteem: They need:

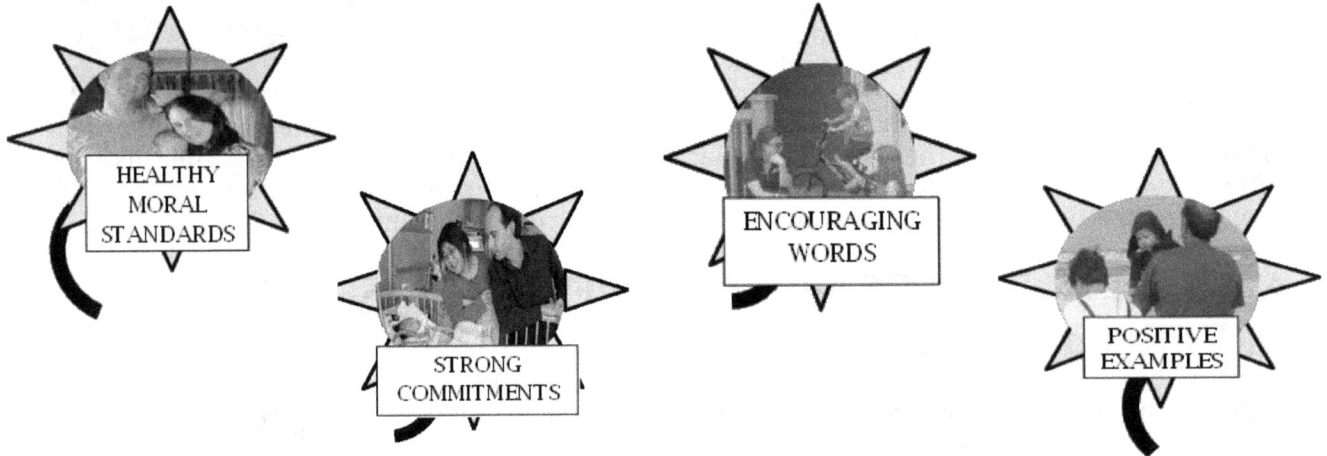

HEALTHY MORAL STANDARDS

STRONG COMMITMENTS

ENCOURAGING WORDS

POSITIVE EXAMPLES

Children are our most precious gift, yet how many parents spend as much time preparing for a child to be born as they do planting a garden? Sadly, most parents don't prepare at all and they just rely on the parenting skills that have been taught by their own parents, which may not have been very good at all. This doesn't mean we don't love our children if we don't know how to be a positive parent, it just means that we need to learn how to become a good role model so we can influence our children in a positive way.

Creating fertile soil and planting good seeds will help our children build confidence and increase their self-worth, giving them a solid base for happiness and future success. Research has proven that if we have just 1 person who supports and loves us, that we will have a much better chance for a secure future. There are so many children and teens today that don't have a good role model to follow. We should all try to be a good example so we can influence at least one person in our lives. Be that 1 person who can make a difference.

What kinds of seeds have been planted in your garden? Have people planted positive or negative seeds? Are you planting positive or negative seeds?

In order to make our garden of life beautiful, we have to make sure we are planting positive seeds, both in ourselves and in others. If you feel that your life was planted with negative seeds, don't be disheartened, you can always make changes that will help your garden flourish by planting your own positive seeds. Of course, negative seeds will always fall into your garden because this world is full of negativity, but you can keep them under control with a lot of work and patience. Now is the time to take action and start planting those positive seeds so they will start growing.

THE SEED GROWS

When a seed is ready to grow, it starts to poke through the ground. When it is time for a baby to be born, the mother makes the necessary preparations. Soon the baby will be removed from its secure home, smacked on the bottom, handed from person to person and left alone in a small bed.

THE BABY CRIES OUT FOR ATTENTION!

- I am afraid
- I am lonely
- I am confused
- I am hungry
- I want attention
- **LISTEN TO ME!!**

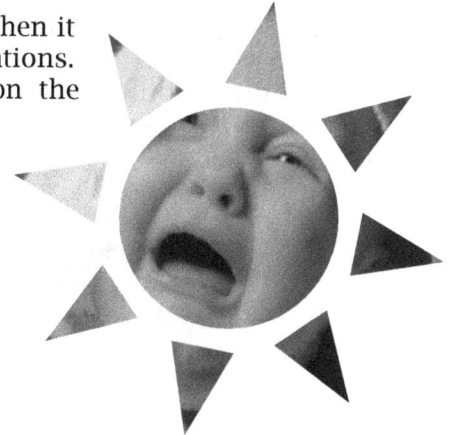

Doesn't this sound like many adults today? "I want this. I need that. Why aren't you listening to me?" So what has changed since childhood? Unfortunately for many people, they have not learned how to develop confidence and they struggle with low self-worth.

Babies are born naturally self-centred. Everything is 'I' or 'me'. The world revolves around them. Without proper direction and guidance, children will grow into selfish adults with a negative mindset.

As the baby grows, it learns basic skills. Everything it hears and sees will have an effect on its emotional, mental, social and spiritual growth. The way we treat a child and other people around us will have an effect on the child's personality. We need to be positive role models and teach them proper behaviours.

If we haven't been treated properly as a child, it will affect how we feel about ourselves and how we treat our children. It is important that we start building our own confidence and have a strong sense of worth, so we can become a good role model to others. It is never too late to change and we are never too old to learn.

What kind of role model are you? We don't want to be a model of an angry, bitter or nasty person. This certainly doesn't help anyone, especially ourselves, and it won't attract friends. People want to be around those who are happy, friendly and sincere.

- ➤ If we model love, people will learn to love.
- ➤ If we model patience, people will learn to be patient.
- ➤ If we model kindness, people will learn to be kind.
- ➤ If we model responsibility, people will learn to be responsible.

We need to build good habits ourselves and become a positive role model so we can help our children and influence everyone around us in a positive way. By providing our children with a loving, supportive atmosphere, they will develop the skills necessary to overcome life's challenges and difficulties.

Train up a child in the way he should go; even when he is old he will not depart from it. Proverbs 22:6

CHILDREN NEED TO BE MOLDED

When a potter is ready to create a new piece of pottery, a piece of clay is selected and put on a potter's wheel. Then it is carefully molded into something of beauty which is put into an oven and dried until it is hardened and ready to display or use. God is the master potter and He created us to become something beautiful and worthy.

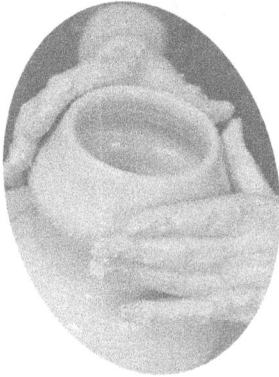

- Babies are like a lump of clay that is waiting to be molded into something beautiful – a unique individual.

- Shaping clay is a delicate process.

- Shaping a child is also a delicate process and both need to be handled with care or they can become damaged or broken.

> But now, O LORD, thou art our father; we are the clay, and thou our potter; and we all are the work of thy hand. Isaiah 64:8

As soon as a baby is born, it starts learning and we need to show them how important and special they are. By treating them and others with kindness and respect, it will teach them how to become a confident, caring individual.

Words and actions speak loudly in their small world and will remain with them as their world grows. We always need to think carefully about what we say and do because someone might be watching us. Young children are great imitators and they will try to imitate the actions of everyone around them. You might notice a child imitating a bad behaviour that you have shown them without even realizing it. We aren't always aware of what we are doing because we do many things by habit, but all of us have bad habits that we know are wrong and if we don't actively change them, we may have a bad influence on the people around us.

Most people have heard the expression, "**Sticks and stones may break my bones, but words will never hurt me**". The person that created this statement obviously didn't understand the power of words. Just a few unkind words can affect people in a negative way and cause destruction in their lives.

- **Words can heal or words can hurt.**
- **Words can stop conflict or start conflict.**
- **Words can build up or tear down.**

It is so important to be careful what we say to others and also what we say to ourselves. Once a word is spoken or written, it can never be taken back. Any negative words or actions can cause immediate damage that will be hard to repair. Always try to use positive words and actions.

WHICH OF THE FOLLOWING WOULD BE POSITIVE FOR A CHILD TO SEE AND HEAR?

HUGS		ENCOURAGING WORDS		ABUSIVE PUNISHMENTS
SAYING 'THANKS'		ARGUING PARENTS		SMILES
READING THE BIBLE		DRINKING EXCESSIVELY		SHARING TOYS
SAYING 'GO AWAY'		HELPING CLEAN ROOM		GIVING A GIFT
IGNORING THEM		GOING TO THE PARK		SMOKING

Answers are found on the answer page at the back of the book.

> O God, thou art my God; early will I seek thee: my soul thirsteth for thee, my flesh longeth for thee in a dry and thirsty land, where no water is,   Psalm 63:1

What would happen if we didn't water our gardens? Water is a basic need for all living things, so without it, everything in a garden would wither and die.

People also need water along with other basic needs of food, shelter and clothing. Without proper nutrition and care, they would likely get sick and possibly die. We need to ensure that our children are cared for properly so they will be able to grow and flourish.

Another basic need for children and all humans is emotional nutrition, which includes love and attention. We can EXIST without it, but we cannot LIVE without it. Research shows that children who do not receive love are emotionally deprived and this can have tragic results. This includes children who are ignored, abused, neglected or disrespected. They can fail to thrive and end up with medical and developmental problems. This results in them becoming adults with:

- ➢ Insecurities & fears
- ➢ Anger, resentment & bitterness
- ➢ Relationship issues
- ➢ A general inability to cope with life

So how can we get emotional nutrition? Let's think of our bodies as emotional tanks. A tank is a *'receptacle for holding or storing something*". Our bodies already store water, but we can imagine it as a holding tank for emotions.

Every day, we put hundreds of emotions into our emotional tanks, both positive and negative. Unfortunately, humans tend to fill themselves with more negative than positive emotions which can have disastrous results.

What happens when we fill our emotional tank with positive emotions?
- ➢ Positive perspective on life, develop good esteem, have stronger relationships, happy

What happens when we fill our emotional tank with negative emotions?
- ➢ Negative perspective on life, have poor esteem, broken relationships, miserable

It's just like when we fill our vehicle with good (positive) fuel. It runs properly. When we fill our vehicle with bad (negative) fuel or no fuel, it won't run properly or will not run at all.

We can't stop negative emotions as they are a part of life, but we can try to fill our emotional tanks with more positive than negative emotions. By having lots of positive emotions in our emotional tanks, we will have a more positive outlook on life and have stronger esteem so we can withstand negative peer pressure, bullying and other forms of personal attacks.

Every day, we need to consciously work on filling our emotional tanks with 'positive fuel'. We can do this in 3 ways:
- • Read scripture verses that remind us how much God loves us and how valuable we are
- • Surround ourselves with positive people/things that will fill our own emotional tanks
- • Fill others with 'positive fuel' so they will be able to help us keep our emotional tank full of 'positive fuel'

> But whosoever drinketh of the water that I shall give him shall never thirst; but the water that I shall give him shall be in him a well of water springing up into everlasting life. John 4:14

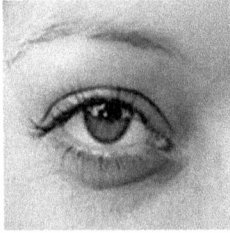

TEASING AND BULLYING

Have you ever been teased or bullied? This is negative fuel and it can have a lifelong effect on you. Teasing is just a mild form of bullying. Teasing is when people poke fun at you and don't really intend to hurt you, but it can still hurt you if you are sensitive. Bullying on the other hand is when someone intentionally tries to hurt you verbally or physically.

Research shows that 1 in 5 Canadian youths are being bullied regularly and 45% of children do not feel safe when they go to school. Bullying has negative effects on everyone and we all need to do what we can to stop this problem.

Why do bullies bully? This is because they have been bullied or abused themselves and they have little control over their lives. By attacking someone who is weaker and has low esteem, they are in control and temporarily feel powerful.

What should you do when you are being bullied? Ignore them, walk away, tell someone, ask God for help. Work on becoming more confident so you can stand up to the bully and firmly tell them to leave you alone. Bullies don't usually bother confident people, they thrive on those who cry or act scared. Never try to insult or threaten the bully as it makes the situation worse.

What should you do if you are the bully? Bullying is a bad habit that is very destructive to everyone. Determine why you have this bad behaviour and find someone who can help you build your esteem. Once you are able overcome your insecurities and fears, you will learn how to accept yourself and not feel the need to bully.

If you see someone that is being bullied, try to step in unless your safety is at risk. Research shows that when a friend steps in to help, bullying stops in 10 seconds or less in many situations. Bullies like an audience, so don't give them one. Stop them dead in their tracks.

Do you think you have the right to hurt someone physically or verbally? Why or why not?
Do you think anyone has the right to hurt you physically or verbally? Why or why not?

When someone hurts us, we naturally feel bad, but we should try to understand why they are hurting us. It may be:
- They just didn't think about what they said
- They were dealing with a difficult situation in their lives
- They were not feeling well
- They were jealous
- They had been hurt by someone else

People who hurt other people are usually hurting themselves in some way but this does not give them the right to hurt us. We have to remind ourselves that they have an issue that needs to be dealt with and we can't change their behaviour. We should remind ourselves that we are valuable and try not to allow their poor behaviour to affect us in a negative way. Ask God to help give you strength to deal with the bullying and pray that He will help the bully to change.

> Think about a situation where someone bullied you or someone else? Briefly describe what happened.
>
>
>
> How could the situation have been handled in a more positive way?

GROWING POSITIVE HABITS

People are creatures of habit. We often do things without even thinking about what we are doing, simply because we have developed a habit.

Since people have a natural tendency to be negative and self-centered, we learn bad habits easily. Good habits can be easy to start, but because they require more time and patience, we lose interest quickly and go back to our old, bad habits.

Research has shown that we can develop a new habit in about 21 to 42 consecutive days and this is why certain programs run for a 3 to 6 week period, although trying to change an old, bad habit with a new, good habit can take longer. After a new habit has been formed, it is important to practice or repeat it to keep reinforcing it.

Take a few moments and think about some new, positive habits that you would like to form or some bad habits that need to be changed or eliminated. Write these in the shapes below.

Pick the habit that you would most like to form or change and write it in your journal for 21 consecutive days starting on a suitable day. Then follow the instructions and after 3 weeks, you will probably be doing this habit automatically. If you are still having trouble, write it down for another 21 days and keep practising it. Then keep maintaining your habit until you do it without thinking. When you feel confident that your habit is well established, start working on another one and keep going.

Here is an example: You have decided that you want to read your Bible every day and spend more time talking to God but you always have some kind of excuse for not doing so. You are too busy, too tired or you simply forget. Try setting an alarm on your phone or writing a reminder for at least 21 days on a calendar and schedule in the time you need.

> **Therefore now amend your ways and your doings, and obey the voice of the LORD your God; and the LORD will repent him of the evil that he hath pronounced against you. Jeremiah 26:13**

If we have carried low esteem into our adulthood, it is extremely important that we learn confidence building skills and make some positive changes. In order to do this we need:

- ✓ To be motivated in making a change from negative to positive
- ✓ To be aware of the steps that need to be taken
- ✓ To learn positive habits and commit to keeping them
- ✓ To be patience and actively work on becoming positive

When new, good habits are formed, our words and actions will become second nature and we will become positive without even thinking about it. We need to learn that:

- ➢ Becoming perfect isn't possible in an imperfect world
- ➢ We **will** make mistakes and that it isn't always our fault
- ➢ Success is possible with the proper guidance and motivation
- ➢ We are all valuable and unique children of God

Replacing bad habits with good habits will improve our physical, mental, emotional and spiritual self.

Good habits will help us overcome:

- ✓ Feelings of worthlessness
- ✓ Fears and insecurities
- ✓ Addictions
- ✓ Poor behaviours
- ✓ Pressures and stresses
- ✓ Depression and anxiety

Positive thinking is a good habit that can be developed with daily practice. Having a positive attitude allows us to look at life with a positive perspective and not let negative people or situations weigh us down. Positive thinking builds confidence and strong esteem.

Do you have a positive or negative perspective on life? Take a look at the following example.

The owner of a cleaning company is curious about the attitude of her employees whom she has never met. She arranges with 3 of her elderly clients to pay a surprise visit to their homes and pretends to be a friend of the family. When she meets the employee, she asks them what kind of work they are doing. Here are the answers she got:

__Employee 1__ seems impatient and answers angrily: 'I'm just the cleaning lady.'
__Employee 2__ seems pleasant enough and answers: 'I'm the cleaning lady and I'm working to support my family.'
__Employee 3__ seems full of joy and answers with a big smile: 'I'm the person who is helping my clients stay in their homes longer. They can't do their cleaning, but I can!'

Clearly, the last employee loved what she was doing and could see how much of an impact it was making on the lives of her clients. She had a positive perspective and was much happier. You **CAN** love what you are doing, no matter what it is, depending on your perspective.

WEEDING & PRUNING YOUR GARDEN

Gardens need to be weeded and pruned in order to gain strength. By taking off dead or weak buds, flowers will grow larger & more beautiful. By trimming weak or small branches, trees will bear sweeter fruit. By thinning out bushes, the result will be thicker and stronger branches.

People also need to have their personalities weeded and pruned in order to gain strength. Negative thoughts, words and actions need to be changed into positive thoughts, words and actions. Everyone around us will feed us positive and negative fuel. We can also feed ourselves positive and negative fuel. This can be done through the food we eat, the words we speak or our actions.

> Every branch in me that beareth not fruit he taketh away: and every branch that beareth fruit, he purgeth it, that it may bring forth more fruit. John 15:2

POSITIVE FUEL is the good things that fill us up and give us confidence. This can include:

- Nourishing food
- Positive comments
- Encouragement & support
- Love & appreciation
- Happy situations
- Family rated movies
- Inspirational books & music
- Acts of kindness
- Talking with friends
- Family time
- Attending church
- Family scripture reading
- Family prayer time
- Gentle touch, hugs

FRUIT & VEGGIE

A GREAT JOB!

FAMILY REUNION

NICE TRY!

A KIND WORD

WATCH MARY POPPINS

NEGATIVE FUEL is the bad things that fill us up and destroy our confidence. This can include:

- Unhealthy or junk food
- Negative comments
- Neglect or abuse
- Unhappy situations
- Viewing pornography
- Being nasty to others
- Being ignored
- Abandonment
- Gossip & rumours
- Bullying
- Getting hurt/hurting others

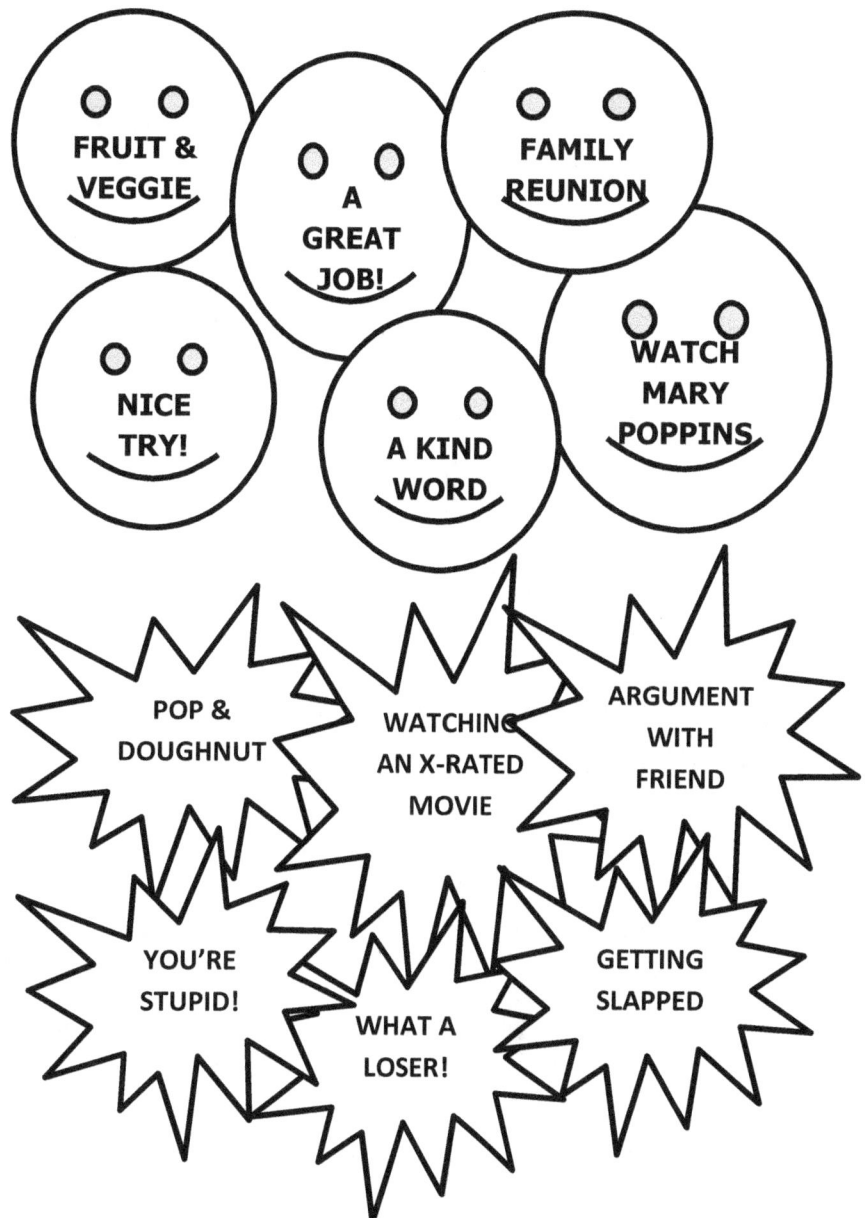

POP & DOUGHNUT

WATCHING AN X-RATED MOVIE

ARGUMENT WITH FRIEND

YOU'RE STUPID!

WHAT A LOSER!

GETTING SLAPPED

POSITIVE AND NEGATIVE FUEL

Many of us are like the characters in the Wizard of Oz, believing the lies that people tell us instead of the truth God has given us in The Bible. For example, if someone tells us we are 'stupid, weak or unlovable', the words go in our ears, get processed by our brain and go directly into our heart where they can stick like a thorn. These words are 'negative fuel' and will create problems for us unless we have a large amount of 'positive fuel' on hand. We have to stop believing everything that people say to us and have confidence in ourselves.

We will always have people and situations that fill us with negative fuel, so we have to make sure that we fill ourselves and others with lots of positive fuel. Following are some positive and negative statements. Put a checkmark in the appropriate box.
Answers are found on the answer page at the back of the book.

		POSITIVE	NEGATIVE
1	My life is a failure.		
2	Why do I bother trying to find a job, nobody will hire me anyway.		
3	I'm a great person.		
4	The situation is hopeless, I should just stop trying.		
5	I always feel sick.		
6	Today is going to be a good day.		
7	I'm a hard worker and always do my best.		
8	I look like a freak, no wonder I don't have any friends.		
9	I had fries and onion rings for lunch.		
10	I like my new outfit, it makes me feel good.		
11	I'm a nice person and people usually like me.		
12	I'm too fat, so there is no point dieting.		
13	My friends gave me a special party for my birthday.		
14	I gained 2 lbs this week, but I lost 3 lbs last week.		
15	I'm a unique and special person.		
16	I have talents that I can share with others.		
17	I like to help people learn new activities.		
18	I'm just too stupid to learn anything new.		

Finally, brethren, whatsoever things are true, whatsoever things are honest, whatsoever things are just, whatsoever things are pure, whatsoever things are lovely, whatsoever things are of good report; if there be any virtue, and if there be any praise, think on these things.
Philippians 4:8

POSITIVE AND NEGATIVE SELF-TALK

People often talk to themselves in a negative way. We are definitely '**our own worst enemies**', and we often say things to ourselves that we would never say to others. These negative words can become our beliefs and will stick with us for the rest of our lives unless we make changes.

Negative self-talk can destroy our confidence and create problems in our relationships. We talk ourselves into being unworthy of anyone's love, incapable of doing anything good and unable to accomplish anything of value. Our words can cut like **SWORDS** into our very soul and destroy any possibility of happiness or success in our lives.

Changing the way we talk requires an awareness of what we are actually saying. Unfortunately, most people who use negative self-talk don't even realize how they are talking. Unless another individual brings it to their attention, it will often go unnoticed.

In order to change negative self-talk, it is necessary to determine why you have this bad habit. For many people, it originates in their childhood and having a family pattern of criticism and conflict. For others, it could be from a more recent abusive relationship. It could also stem from being over-immersed in the media, which portrays unrealistic images of beauty and gives the false message that people need possessions to be happy and successful.

When the source is discovered, steps need to be taken to **replace the negative self-talk with positive self-talk. Following are some steps to take:**

1) Write your self-talk in a daily journal
   • Evaluate what you have written - are your words true or are they what others say about you and judge you to be
   • Rewrite your self-talk by replacing the negative words with positive words
2) Every day look carefully at yourself in a mirror
   • Say positive things about yourself
   • Always smile at yourself
   • Tell yourself you look good
   • How would God see you in the mirror?
3) Use positive affirmations
   • Write these on coloured shapes and put on your fridge or mirrors – read them out loud every time you see them
   • Write them on index cards and carry in your purse or pocket – take them out several times each day and read them (out loud if possible)
   • Affirm others with positive statements – it will make them feel good and provide you with a warm feeling of contentment
4) Focus on the positives
   • When a negative thought comes into your mind, stop yourself and think about something positive
   • Ask yourself what God would think

> Casting down imaginations, and every high thing that exalteth itself against the knowledge of God, and bringing into captivity every thought to the obedience of Christ;
> 2 Corinthians 10:5

Changing your self-talk will require a lot of time and effort but the results are well worth it. By spending time each day working towards your goal, you will soon have created a good habit that will be hard to break.

HOW DO YOU TALK TO YOURSELF?

Get started on changing your self-talk by replacing these negative statements with positive statements. The first one has been done to show you how.

I always make mistakes. I can't ever do anything right.
→Sometimes I make mistakes, but I try hard and usually do things right.
I'm so depressed and I don't feel like getting out of bed.
→
I'm too stupid to learn that, so no point trying.
→
I'm so dumb. I'll never get this job.
→
I'm too fat and I need to lose about 50 lbs.
→
Nobody likes me, so I might as well stay home.
→
I'm not going to the party. Nobody will talk to me anyway.
→
I don't think I'll ever get married. I'm just too ugly and stupid.
→
Let the words of my mouth, and the meditation of my heart, be acceptable in thy sight, O LORD, my strength, and my redeemer. Psalms 19:14
Pleasant words are as a honeycomb, sweet to the soul, and health to the bones. Proverbs 16:24

CONTINUOUS CARE IN YOUR GARDEN

If you want to maintain a beautiful garden, it is necessary to keep caring for it on a continuous basis, even at times when things are looking good or appear to be lying dormant for a while.

People also need to be cared for on a continuous basis even if they seem to be doing well, so they will always feel loved and appreciated. Even the most confident person can be overwhelmed when difficulties and unpleasant situations arise. This is when caring support is needed the most.

Learn what kind of love language people have so you can make sure they are getting what they need. Some feel loved when you spend time with them, give them a small gift or just give them a hug. Others feel loved when you do something nice for them or tell them how much you appreciate them. Your love language won't be the same as another person, so make sure you give them what they need so their garden will continue to bloom and grow.

You can also provide yourself with continuous care by keeping your emotional tank full and overflowing with positive fuel. Other people are not always available when you need support, so you need to **feed yourself with positive self-talk every day and use positive affirmations.** There are several affirming scripture verses located in this workbook that are uplifting, encouraging and reassuring. Write them down, add more of your own and read them often.

You can also help others fill their emotional tanks by talking to them in a positive way, praying for them and doing nice things for them. This has a double effect – it helps them and also you.

Volunteering is a good way of spreading joy around. Every community has numerous organizations and churches that could use your special skills and talents for a few hours a month or even once or twice a year.

It has been proven that volunteering has significant physical and mental health benefits including:
- Decrease in stress
- Less pain
- Reduction of negative attitudes
- Improved emotional well-being
- Combats depression
- Reduced risk of cardiovascular disease and diabetes
- Lower cholesterol levels
- Strengthening of the immune system
- Helps you make new friends and contacts
- Increases your social skills
- Better communication
- Improved task management and organization
- Increases confidence and strengthens esteem
- Provides career experience
- Teaches you valuable job skills
- Enjoying hobbies and interests

Take a look in your phone book or look up agencies on the internet and pick one that you would be interested in working for (people, animals, causes). _____

Bear ye one another's burdens, and so fulfil the law of Christ. Galatians 6:2

WHAT IS IN YOUR GARDEN?

What would people see in your garden?
- ➤ Beautiful flowers with bright, vivid colours
- ➤ Thick trees with ripe, juicy fruit
- ➤ Full bushes and healthy plants

Or would they see.......
- ➤ Wilting and drooping flowers
- ➤ Dead and brittle branches
- ➤ Ugly weeds
- ➤ Rotting leaves and debris

A garden isn't made beautiful by just sitting and looking at it. Action is required.

It would probably be a combination of beautiful and dead flowers, healthy plants and ugly weeds. In the space below there are flowers and weeds. Which ones are found in your garden? Circle them.

A HELPING HAND	ANGER	HAPPINESS	BITTERNESS	PEACE
HURTFUL COMMENTS	SWEET SMILES	COMPLAINTS	CARING THOUGHTS	GROUCHINESS
KINDNESS	RUDENESS	COMPASSION	SHARP WORDS	PLEASANT CONVERSATION

Count the number of pretty flowers._____ Count the number of ugly weeds._____

There will always be some weeds in our garden, but we need to keep working on eliminating them so we can maintain a healthy lifestyle. More people are attracted to a beautiful garden than a patch of weeds, so if we want our relationships to flourish, we need to work hard on becoming that beautiful garden.

If your personal garden of life is not as healthy as you would like it to be:

- • ask God to help you determine what is missing
- • review the steps needed to create a beautiful garden
- • make a plan and start growing

The grass is only greener on the other side of the fence if they are taking better care of it. Try taking good care of your own grass and it will also be green.

THE BUTTERFLY EMERGES PART THREE
A Journey into Self-Image

If a stranger asked you to briefly describe your looks, personality and abilities in a letter, what would you say?

Dear Stranger,
My name is Matt. I'm 6 feet tall with short brown hair and brown eyes. I play basketball and have made lots of goals this year. My body is well-toned and I lift weights. My grades are excellent, I write for the school paper and everyone loves me. I'm a real party animal!

OR

Dear Stranger,
My name is Matt. I'm about 6 feet tall. My hair is sort of brown and sticks out around my ears which are too big. I'm a bit skinny but am working on building some muscles. I'm doing okay in school but I have trouble making friends because people are always making fun of me.

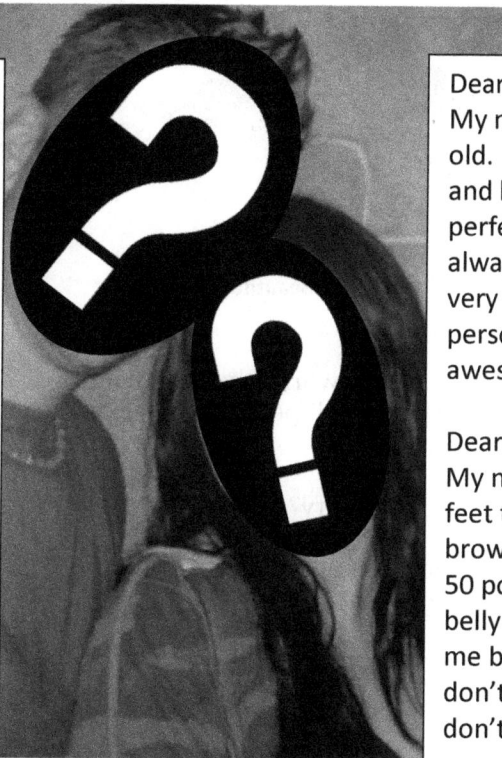

Dear Stranger,
My name is Barb. I'm 18 years old. I have gorgeous brown hair and beautiful eyes. I am a perfect size 5 and my clothing is always the latest fashion. I'm a very talented singer with a great personality and have tons of awesome friends.

OR

Dear Stranger,
My name is Barb. I'm just over 5 feet tall. My hair is sort of brown and straggly. I'm about 50 pounds overweight and my belly sticks out. Nobody likes me because I look like a freak. I don't blame them because I don't like myself either.

The 2 descriptions of Matt and Barb are describing the same person but they sound like 2 different people. The first descriptions show too much confidence and the second descriptions show no confidence at all. The honest description should be somewhere in the middle.

Part 3 will take you on a journey into your self-image. It will help you understand what real beauty is, uncover some important truths about yourself and show you how to develop your inner and outer beauty. Looking at yourself with a positive perspective will give you added confidence and boost your esteem.

Beauty is certainly a gift and it comes to different people in different ways. Some people have beautiful skin or eyes; others have beautiful personalities or beautiful talents, qualities and skills. God has given us special gifts and we should treat them with care and respect. But how many of us treat ourselves as a special gift?

- Do you appreciate the gifts you have been given or do you want someone else's gifts?
- Do you take care of your gifts or use them inappropriately?
- Do you use your gifts as best you can or do you try to ignore them or keep them hidden?

Many of us don't value ourselves for who we are and sometimes we don't even see our own beauty and strength.

If you were asked to think of some things that were beautiful, what would you picture in your mind?

Beautiful movie star	Beautiful new home	Beautiful new shoes	Beautiful scenery	Beautiful baby

There are all sorts of things in the world that are beautiful. However, everyone has a different idea of what beauty is and this can depend on where we came from (our country of origin) and the environment we grew up in.

But what is the real meaning of beauty? The dictionary states that beauty is:

- Pleasing and impressive qualities of something
- Pleasing personal appearance
- A fine example
- An excellent aspect

This means that in order to be beautiful, we must have good looks or good qualities. It does NOT say that we have to have the PERFECT figure, flawless skin and expensive clothing. This idea comes from a universal image that is put in our minds through the media so they can sell products and services. Both men and women have a twisted concept about what real beauty is and this creates most of our issues with self-worth and body confidence.

Real beauty comes from knowing who we are in Christ and being able to see our true value.
Beauty is not just how we look on the outside, it comes from inside and reflects a beautiful character. Inner beauty can literally be a light that shines brightly from the inside out.

> But the LORD said to Samuel, "Do not look on his appearance or on the height of his stature, because I have rejected him. For the LORD sees not as man sees: man looks on the outward appearance, but the LORD looks on the heart." 1 Samuel 16:7

SURROUND YOURSELF WITH BEAUTIFUL PEOPLE

It is important to surround yourself with beautiful people if you want to feel beautiful yourself. This does not mean you should look for people who are physically attractive. Beauty is not just about our outer appearance, it is a combination of our inner and outer self. Truly beautiful people are those who have inner beauty that shines through and reflects their entire being.

Inner beauty includes the following:
- Good personality
- Integrity
- Good manners
- Respect
- Charm
- Good taste
- Intelligence
- Kindness
- Positive attitude
- Confidence and strong esteem

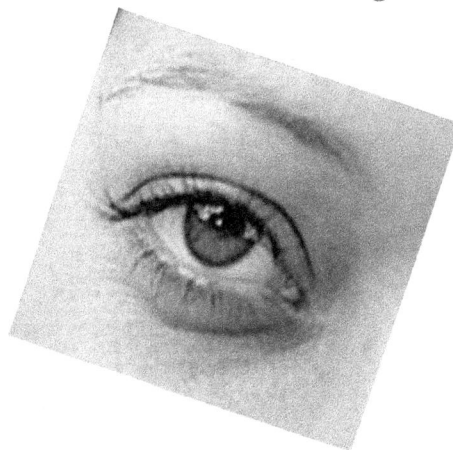

Outer beauty includes the following:
- Being well-groomed and neatly dressed
- Having pleasing physical attributes (shiny hair, clean skin, sparking eyes)
- Caring actions, helping others
- Friendly smiles
- Being a positive example
- Showing a reflection of your inner beauty

If you surround yourself with people who have many of these characteristics, their influence will provide you with positive energy and help you feel good about yourself. The opposite is also true; if you surround yourself with people who have few or none of these characteristics, their influence will provide you with negative energy and make you feel bad about yourself.

Think about the friends you have. Make a list of up to 10 your closest friends below.

☺		☺	
☺		☺	
☺		☺	
☺		☺	
☺		☺	

Do these friends make you feel good or bad?

It is nice to have lots of friends but it is better to have just 1 good friend than 25 bad friends. Good friends are hard to find and sometimes we think that a bad friend is better than no friend at all, but this is very wrong. A bad friend can cause a lot of problems in our lives and completely destroy our self-worth.

WHO ARE YOUR REAL FRIENDS?

How can you tell if a friend is a good friends or a bad friend? Try the quiz below. Choose your best friend and HONESTLY answer the questions below with a yes or no.

		YES	NO
1	We trust each other completely.		
2	We like to spend time together.		
3	My friend makes me feel good about myself.		
4	We share secrets that are not repeated to anyone.		
5	We disagree but can still talk about things.		
6	We encourage each other.		
7	We have fun being together.		
8	We stick up for each other when someone tries to hurt us.		
9	We are always there for each other even when we are sick or hurt.		
10	We accept each other's differences.		

If you answered all the questions with 'YES', then you likely have a good friend that you can count on no matter what happens.
If you answered a mixture of 'YES' and 'NO', you need to be cautious because your friend is lacking in some important traits of a good friend.
If you answered all the questions with 'NO', this is not a good friend, you won't be able to count on them and they will likely hurt you.
Try this quiz with all your other friends, than try it on yourself. Are you a good friend?

We all want people to like us and it is important that we have friends, but we really need to choose our friends carefully. Certainly, none of us are perfect either, but we should never allow anyone else to hurt us, especially those we consider to be our friends.

OUR INNER AND OUTER CIRCLE

We should all have an inner and outer circle of friends.
- The inner circle should just include 1 or a few close family members or friends that you totally trust.
- The outer circle should include all the other people that you know; those who are negative or those who aren't very close to you at all.

Who is in YOUR inner and outer circle? You really need to take a close look at who you know and determine if in fact they are real, true friends. There may be some friends in your inner circle that you really can't count on and these should be moved to your outer circle. This doesn't mean you should totally ignore them, it means that you need to distance yourself from them until they either become a better friend or until you are strong enough to have a positive influence on them.

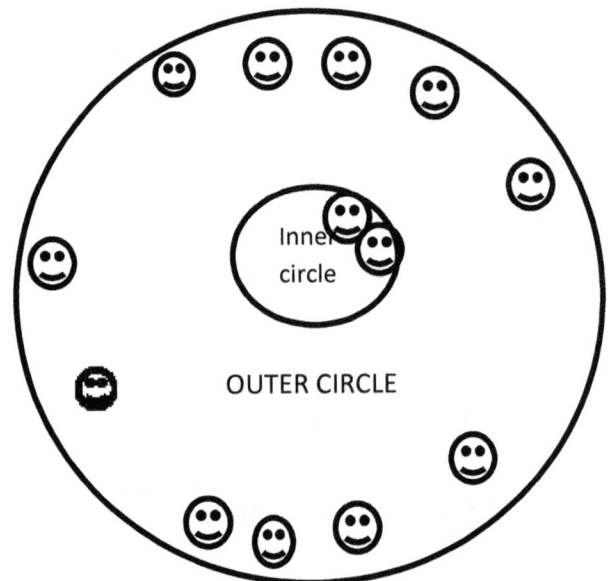

FEELING BEAUTIFUL

How would you feel if I told you I liked your outfit and that you were the best looking person in this room?

Would you take it as a compliment and feel good about yourself?

Would you be upset and wonder why I was being nice to you?

Would you be embarrassed and want to hide?

Everyone reacts differently when receiving a compliment. **People who have confidence** in their self-image will feel good. **People who lack trust** in others may think there is an ulterior motive. **People who have low esteem** will not believe the praise is true.

In order for anyone to feel beautiful, they must be confident and love themselves the way God loves them (not in a selfish or harmful way). They must nourish all areas of their being – their minds, their bodies, their soul and their spirit. Many people tend to concentrate on only 1 or 2 areas and neglect the others, thus defeating total success.

Feeling beautiful helps you maintain confidence, which will promote YOU when it comes to relationships, work and finding your purpose in life.

Do you feel beautiful and confident in any of the following areas?
☐ face   ☐ hair   ☐ skin   ☐ clothing   ☐ body   ☐ style   ☐ actions   ☐ presence   ☐ speaking

Do you feel the need to improve in any of the following areas?
☐ face   ☐ hair   ☐ skin   ☐ clothing   ☐ body   ☐ style   ☐ actions   ☐ presence   ☐ speaking

What area is the biggest concern to you? _____

Ideally, you should feel confident about your self-image and not feel the need to improve in any area. However, most people struggle with certain areas of their appearance or how they present themselves. Building and keeping strong esteem is something we all need to keep working on.

Try doing this exercise again in a few weeks or months when you feel your esteem is better and see if there are any changes.

> **As the Father hath loved me, so have I loved you: continue ye in my love.**
> **John 15:9**

PERSONAL HYGIENE

Cleanliness is important to good health and if neglected can cause a lot of problems. If you don't look and smell good, you will have problems in your everyday life. Every part of your body needs to have attention on a regular basis.

Personal hygiene is how you look after your external body. The ancient Greeks were very aware of the importance of hygiene and they spent hours in the bath, using fragrances and make-up to beautify their bodies so they would be presentable to others.

Beauty products are sold by many companies and are endorsed by high profile celebrities, creating a billion dollar market. They promote their products as a necessity for confidence, while in actual fact they only provide a superficial confidence that lasts as long as the products are being used.

The only successful way to build real and lasting confidence is by caring for our bodies the way God intended us to. If we keep our bodies clean, well-nourished and fit, we will be healthy and be able to promote our self-image in a positive way. In the next few pages, we will give you some basic guidelines for staying healthy.

> What? Know ye not that your body is the temple of the Holy Ghost which is in you, which ye have of God, and ye are not your own? For ye are bought with a price: therefore glorify God in your body, and in your spirit, which are God's. 1 Corinthians 6:19-20

DAILY WASHING

The body has almost 2 million sweat glands that produce up to a pint of sweat each day. In order to minimize problems from bacteria, it is important to wash daily with soap and water to keep your skin clean.

Take a shower or a bath and if you are very active in sports or have an active job, it might be necessary to take more than one on the days of higher activity.

Use the following items: mild soap, washcloth or bath sponge, back brush, heel scrubber

Clean all areas of your body thoroughly, especially your private areas as natural secretions can cause irritation and infection if left unclean.

Rinse off all soap carefully to avoid leaving excess residue that will dry out your skin. Use a clean towel and dry your skin completely.

Use deodorant or an antiperspirant and put on clean underwear and clothing. If you have any allergies or rashes, check with a doctor to see if there are special products you can use to avoid body odour.

SOME QUIZZES

DO YOU HAVE GOOD OR POOR HYGIENE?

Answer by circling yes or no.

1) Should you wash your hands each time you use the washroom?	Yes	No
2) Should you only use your own personal soap?	Yes	No
3) Should you put the lid down on the toilet after using it and before flushing?	Yes	No
5) Should you carry kleenex or a handkerchief?	Yes	No
6) Should you carry hand sanitizer?	Yes	No
7) Should you use deodorant or anti-perspirant every day?	Yes	No
8) Should you let animals lick your face?	Yes	No
9) Should you bring your own utensils to a public place to eat with?	Yes	No
10) Should you use the comb of a friend?	Yes	No
11) Should you use a friend's makeup?	Yes	No
12) Should you eat a candy that fell on the floor?	Yes	No
13) Should you use someone else's toothbrush?	Yes	No
14) Should you drink out of someone else's glass?	Yes	No

HOW OFTEN? Below are 4 questions. Circle your answer or fill in the slot.

1) How often should you get dental checkups?

        twice a year   every year   every 2 years   other _____

2) How often should you take a shower? daily weekly monthly other _____

3) How often should you brush your teeth?

        once daily twice daily after each meal   other _____

4) How often should you wash your sheets? weekly monthly other _____

WHEN SHOULD YOU WASH YOUR HANDS?

OFTEN is the correct answer but there are specific situations where it is extremely important to wash your hands. Check off the appropriate answers.

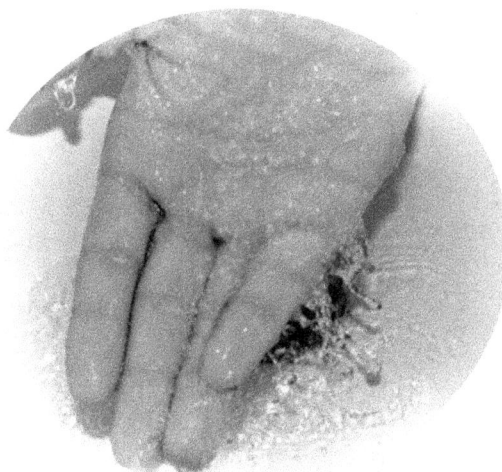

- ☐ Before eating
- ☐ After eating
- ☐ Before getting dressed
- ☐ After touching animals
- ☐ When preparing food
- ☐ After shopping
- ☐ Before and after visiting a sick friend
- ☐ After taking out the garbage
- ☐ When turning on the TV
- ☐ After putting on your shoes
- ☐ After cleaning the toilet
- ☐ After reading a book
- ☐ Before going to bed

Answers are found on the answer page at the back of the book.

HAIR

According to a study done at Yale University, having **'a bad hair day'** causes negative feelings about how we look which directly impacts our esteem. This indicates how important it is to find a style that suits us and is easy to maintain.

The most important thing about hair is to keep it clean and healthy. Here are some basic guidelines:

> - Wash your hair as often as necessary to keep it clean. Normal hair should be done every 2-3 days. Oily hair may need daily washing. Dry hair may be left for a week.
> - Use a mild shampoo and conditioner. Damaged hair may require additional moisturizers.
> - Rinse hair well to remove all residues.
> - Comb wet hair or use a special brush to avoid breakage.
> - Air-dry your hair if possible or use a low heat setting on a dryer to prevent hair damage.
> - Get hair cut regularly to keep it looking good and to eliminate damaged ends.
> - Be careful when colouring or perming hair as these can cause skin allergies, throat infections and hair damage.

It is also important to choose the proper hairstyle. When considering a style, don't just choose one that looks good on someone else – it may not look good on you. Make your own decision and don't rely on what others may say. Even a professional may suggest a style that is not comfortable for you. Do some research, ask for suggestions and then combine these with your own thoughts.

> **But even the very hairs of your head are all numbered. Fear not therefore: ye are of more value than many sparrows. Luke 12:7**

Consider the following:

1. <u>Personality</u> - Are you conservative or outrageous? Do you want to attract attention or just blend in with the scenery? Make sure your style suits your personality so you will feel comfortable with yourself.
2. <u>Physical Attributes</u> – The style should suit your age, weight, hair texture, skin colour, shape of your head and other body features.
3. <u>Cost</u> – Hair should be inexpensive to maintain. Short hair is cut every 4-6 weeks and long hair should be trimmed every 3 months. Perms, colouring and bleaches need to be done every few weeks.
4. <u>Time</u> – Make sure you have time to maintain the style you choose. Busy people need one that is quick and easy.
5. <u>Ability</u> – You should be able to easily recreate the same style.

The best way to find a style that suits your personality, colouring and lifestyle is to connect with a good beauty salon. It may take several tries to find a style or hair salon that works for you, but once you find the right one, you will feel more comfortable and confident.

If you have a healthy body, you will have healthy nails. Brittle or discoloured nails will show if you have any deficiencies or disease conditions.

The best way to care for your nails is through a proper diet and grooming. Eating foods with the daily recommended amount of Vitamin B, Calcium and Protein will help your nails and your entire body to stay healthy. Watch the foods you eat and take a daily multivitamin to ensure you are getting the proper amounts of all the vitamins your body needs.

How to care for nails:
- Keep your nails clean and cut regularly
- Soak hands in warm water to clean and soften
- Dry thoroughly with a clean towel
- Clip nails short, but not too close to the skin
- Long nails are more work and need to be kept very clean
- Clip nails in a rounded or squared shape, avoiding pointed nails as they will likely break off
- Soften and trim cuticles
- Moisturize nail beds daily when possible with a moisturizing lotion so nails won't dry out
- Wear gloves when cleaning, gardening and doing other messy chores to keep clean and avoid breakage

When using nail polish, keep these things in mind:
- Polish causes keratin, of which nails are made, to split
- Give your nails a break as often as possible so they won't dry out
- Keep your nails clean – it is easy to miss dirt under nails that are painted
- When working around food, make sure your nail polish isn't chipping and going into the food
- Avoid using acrylic nails as they can damage your natural nails

If it is possible, have a professional manicure and/or pedicure done every few weeks, especially if you experience any nail problems or if you are a diabetic.

USE MAKEUP SPARINGLY The natural look is the most attractive but few women have naturally beautiful skin so many women use makeup to cover their flaws. Beautiful, healthy skin is not always a reflection of the products you use. Products can cover up flaws and enhance beauty, but they can also give you a false sense of confidence. Also when makeup is applied incorrectly or too heavily, it can actually make a person look worse or even cause skin irritations.

Basic skin care combined with a minimum of makeup can bring out a person's natural beauty. Here are some simple hints:
- Apply a moisturizing cream that matches your skin type – normal, dry or oily
- Use a natural shade of foundation that matches your skin tone – apply sparingly
- Apply blush lightly to your cheeks (can apply to chin and forehead also)
- Apply eye shadow and liner in colours to match your eyes
- Choose lipstick that suits your colouring and compliments the outfit you are wearing

Be cautious when using scented products as they are bad for allergies, breathing problems and skin irritations, not just for yourself, but also for others you come in contact with. Visit your local drugstore and ask the cosmetician what they would recommend. Listen to their advice and use what you feel comfortable with.

SKIN

The best way to care for your skin is having a healthy diet, drinking lots of water, exercising regularly and getting adequate sleep. Using the proper moisturizer and sunscreen is also important.

WATER Experts say we should drink about 8 glasses of water each day. Water re-hydrates your body and helps it detoxify through food digestion and elimination of waste. It increases energy, lubricates joints and carries oxygen to the brain.

How many glasses of water do you drink every day? _____

> But whosoever drinketh of the water that I shall give him shall never thirst; but the water that I shall give him shall be in him a well of water springing up into everlasting life. John 4:14

DIET A proper diet is absolutely necessary for a healthy body. Eating properly is not all that difficult but it does require a change in eating habits. Maintaining a proper, healthy weight is a lifetime commitment. If you have specific health issues that cause problems for your weight, you should discuss a proper diet with your doctor. On page 52, there are some simple suggestions for a healthy diet.

> Every moving thing that liveth shall be meat for you; even as the green herb have I given you all things. Genesis 9:3

EXERCISE You should try to exercise at least 30 minutes a day when possible. Walking is an excellent choice if you can't afford to join a club. When time is a problem, exercise for a few minutes several times a day. Exercise is extremely important as it burns calories, increases energy and improves your physical, mental and emotional life.

How often do you exercise? _____

What kind of exercise do you enjoy doing? _____

> For bodily exercise profiteth little: but godliness is profitable unto all things, having promise of the life that now is, and of that which is to come. 1Timothy 4:8

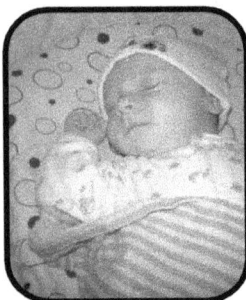

SLEEP Getting enough sleep allows your body to fully recover from any stress it encounters during the day. The average human needs between 7-8 hours of sleep each night. Try to set patterns that will suit your lifestyle and put all your cares out of mind before going to bed. It is never a good idea to go to bed when you are upset, angry or hungry. Any problems should be resolved so you can have a relaxing, restorative sleep.

How many hours of sleep do you get every night? _____

> When thou liest down, thou shalt not be afraid: yea, thou shalt lie down, and thy sleep shall be sweet. Proverbs 3:24

SOME STARTLING STATS

Many people today are addicted to dieting, both men and women. However it seems that women struggle the most because they feel bad about their self-image. Here are some startling statistics on women:

- ➢ By the age of 18, over 80% of women have dieted
- ➢ By the age of 9, about 40% have already dieted
- ➢ Children as young as 5 are known to be dieting

Why do so many young people diet? This is because they don't feel good about their self-image and believe that losing weight will help them become popular and successful. This can be the result of:

- • Constant pressures from the media to be thin
- • Low esteem or other emotional issues
- • Parents/siblings/friends continually dieting or obsessing about their looks

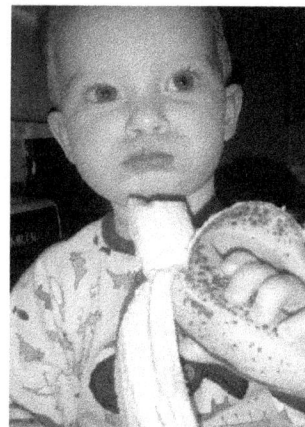

Children get the wrong message when they are surrounded by people who focus on weight loss or how they look. This causes them to believe that their self-image is a priority and the result is a life-long pattern of dieting. Parents and significant others should always try to set a good example and focus on living a healthy lifestyle. When people focus on food, they think about food, but if people focus on healthy eating, they will train themselves to eat properly.

Dieting is a bad habit that we should <u>never</u> allow our children to form.

God tells us that we should enjoy eating but also warns us not to be excessive in eating and drinking.

> And also that every man should eat and drink, and enjoy the good of all his labour, it is the gift of God. Ecclesiastes 3:13
>
> Be not among winebibbers; among riotous eaters of flesh: For the drunkard and the glutton shall come to poverty: Proverbs 23:20-21

Did you grow up in a family who dieted or was obsessed about their looks? Yes☐ No☐

Have you dieted or are you dieting right now? Yes☐ No☐   Explain why you are dieting.

At what age did you start dieting? _____

Has dieting become a problem for you? Yes☐ No☐ How? _____

Do you have an eating disorder? Yes☐ No☐ How does it affect your life? _____

If you are struggling with weight loss or have an eating disorder, **please** visit your family doctor and find out how to stop this bad habit. Your life is valuable and you are the only one who can take care of your health.

DIETING

If you want to maintain a proper, healthy weight it is important to create a regular, long-term plan of action that combines healthy eating with daily exercise.

Unfortunately, people today do not eat healthy foods and they end up gaining a lot of excess weight that can result in health concerns. When this happens, they look for quick and easy ways to lose weight. Unfortunately we didn't gain those extra pounds in a few days or weeks and we can't lose them that fast either.

Think about it, if losing weight and keeping it off were that easy, why are so many people ALWAYS on diets? The fact is 90% of the people on diets WILL FAIL and often they will gain back more weight. Why do something that will likely result in failure?

Most people can lose weight by just cutting back on their food intake and eating healthy foods. Combining this with daily exercise burns calories and keeps your body toned. Add prayer and this will soon become a win-win situation.

Here are some suggestions that might help:

- *When you eat, take your time and eat slowly. Don't rush to eat quickly as it can increase the risk of indigestion and cause acid reflux. It takes about 20 minutes for your brain to acknowledge the fact that you are full.*

- *Never skip meals. People think that skipping meals will help them lose weight but just the opposite is true. When you skip a meal, your metabolism doesn't have to work to break down the food, so it slows down. Then when you do eat something, your metabolism doesn't work as quickly as it should and this results in fat being stored. So instead of losing weight, you are storing fat. Skipping meals also cuts proper nutrition and can promote the development of diabetes.*

- *Eating several small meals a day is actually the best way to maintain a healthy weight and keep your metabolism working properly*

- *Avoid sugar and fried foods. This doesn't mean you can't ever have something sweet or fried. We all need a treat sometimes.*

- *Cut back on caffeine, salt, fatty foods, red meat and eggs. Again you can still have some of these, but not every day.*

- *The best thing to focus on is eating more fruit, vegetables and foods with fiber and calcium. We don't always like healthy foods but you can develop a taste for them if you really want to.*

> **Pray * Eat slowly * Never skip meals * Eat small portions
> Avoid sugar * Cut back on salt * Eat more fruit**

A PICTURE IS WORTH A THOUSAND WORDS. What kind of picture are you showing to the public by the way you dress?

Many people believe that a person is showing their true personality by the way they present themselves. The first thing we do when we meet a person is put a label on them. We look at the clothing they are wearing, their hair style and what kind of accessories they have. Then we listen to how they talk and watch how they act. This quick review gives us our first and often lasting impression of who this person is.

If you passed by the following people, what kind of label would you put on them?

1) Confident Model?   2) Tough Loser?   3) Rich Playboy?   4) Homeless Bum?

Things are not always as they seem. Some of your assumptions may be correct, but they are only assumptions and you don't know the whole truth. **Many of us don't even know who we really are, so how can we judge others?** The labels we put on the pictures may be totally wrong. For example:
1) The confident model may be a not-so-confident lady who is on her way to a job interview and is thinking that someone else will probably get the job.
2) The tough loser might be a successful business owner who is relaxing on vacation at his beach house during a very hot summer.
3) The rich playboy might be someone who has very little money, but is going with some friends to a dinner party wearing a borrowed suit jacket, tie and a hat.
4) The homeless bum might have lost his wife to cancer a month ago and lost everything he had to pay for her medications and funeral, so he now has no home and no money.

Unfortunately, people are often hiding behind masks to cover up flaws and imperfections that they see in themselves and aren't portraying their own personality at all. Many of us are living false lives under the disguise of someone that we want to be, and we are not really showing our true selves to other people. We hide because we think that people won't like us, respect us or accept us for who we are. We hide our real feelings and don't share them with others because they might make fun of us, ignore or gossip about us. This makes us feel imperfect, unworthy and inferior.

Instead of judging others and seeing ourselves through the eyes of the world, we need to start looking at people through God's eyes. We also need to give others a clear picture of who we really are by taking off our own masks and trying to connect with other people in a positive and loving way.

> **Do not judge by appearances, but judge with right judgment. John 7:24**

Remember a time when you got all dressed up to go to a party, wedding or other special occasion. How did you feel? Most people feel pretty good about themselves when they look good.

The type of clothing we wear can have a direct effect on our attitude.

> ➤ If we are dressed in special or expensive clothing, it makes us feel good and important.

> ➤ If we are dressed in casual clothing like jeans and a t-shirt, it makes us feel laid back and relaxed.

> ➤ If we are dressed in dirty work clothes, it makes us feel grubby and wanting to bathe.

Society puts a lot of pressure on people to 'dress for success' by spending money on designer clothing and continually changing to new styles. This can be a costly venture and only open to those who have a lot of money to spend.

When children start school, they are judged on the clothing they wear. This starts them off with a poor image of themselves and they can become obsessed with how they look. Children spend far too much time trying to look good instead of developing confidence and doing well in school.

It is interesting that society urges people to be individuals, yet when we belong to a group, we are pressured into dressing in the same way. Where is the sense in that? If we all look the same, we are basically wearing a uniform and we have no individuality from the others in our group. Perhaps this is a new concept – group individuality?

Everyone is unique and should choose a clothing style that suits their personality. Dressing like someone else will never give you confidence in your own personal image.

Charm is deceitful, and beauty is vain, but a woman who fears the LORD is to be praised. Proverbs 31:30

WHAT DO YOU LIKE?

What is your favourite colour? _____

Do you prefer casual or formal wear? _____

Do you like to dress the same as your friends? _____

How often do you wear the same outfit? _____

What type of clothing stores do you like? _____

A PERSONAL MAKEOVER

Many people could use a Personal Makeover, not just in our outer appearance but also in our inner appearance. This requires an honest look at our unique individuality and determining what changes need to be made. Let's do a makeover in our imagination.

Pretend that you are walking down a street and you pass a man holding a bowl and begging for money. He is dressed in torn blue jeans, a dirty shirt and worn out shoes. His long beard is tangled and you can smell his body odour. What opinion would you have of this person? Write your thoughts in the space below.

Now, pretend it is the next day and you are walking down the same street. You see a nice-looking, clean-cut man standing by a newspaper stand. He is wearing nice clothing and shoes. He smiles and says hello. What opinion would you have of this person? Write your thoughts in the space below.

Naturally, you would have formed 2 different opinions about these 2 people. But what if these 2 people were actually only 1 person? The man just changed his outer clothing and shaved his beard, but inside there was no change at all. In our eyes we saw 2 different people, but to the man, he was the same person today and yesterday.

People can put on different clothing, but this just changes us superficially and doesn't usually affect our real personality. So **what we see is not always necessarily what is true, so we should never judge people by the way they dress.**

However, the way we look can have a profound effect on how others see us and also how we see ourselves. Before going out in the world, ask yourself what image you want others to see. **Always try to look your best**. This will help you feel more comfortable, be confident and see things in a more positive light. Changing our style of dress can have some positive changes in our relationships, at our place of work and affect our attitude towards life.

Visit some clothing stores and ask a clerk to help you decide what clothing styles suit you best. Keep in mind that the price tag or brand name doesn't define who you are. If cost is an issue, there are several discount and second hand stores that carry new and nearly new clothing at good prices. Sometimes you can even find a brand new, brand name clothing item at a used clothing store! Go with a friend and have fun!

> **My brethren, have not the faith of our Lord Jesus Christ, the Lord of glory, with respect of persons. For if there come unto your assembly a man with a gold ring, in goodly apparel, and there come in also a poor man in vile raiment; And ye have respect to him that weareth the gay clothing, and say unto him, Sit thou here in a good place; and say to the poor, Stand thou there, or sit here under my footstool: Are ye not then partial in yourselves, and are become judges of evil thoughts? James 2:1-4**

THE BUTTERFLY EMERGES
PART FOUR
Goal Setting

THE THEORY OF SETTING GOALS BEGAN IN THE LATE 1960'S BY DR EDWIN LOCKE.

He determined that when individuals worked towards specific goals, they were motivated to accomplish their goal and this had a direct impact on how they performed a task. Working towards non-specific goals did not provide motivation and made it harder to reach their goals.

Most successful people set goals and work hard to reach these goals. They don't wait for things to happen to them; instead they make things happen in their lives. They create a plan that will help them reach their ultimate goal in life through a series of short-term plans and tasks.

Goal planning isn't difficult. Even children should start by setting simple goals and be encouraged to work towards them. Goals can be set for a week, month, year or even a lifetime depending on the person's age and capabilities. Goals give purpose to life. They bring together your thoughts and put them into a game plan that you can follow.

PART FOUR will take you on a journey into your thoughts, help you discover your goals in life and get you started on making a plan of action.

> Go to the ant, thou sluggard; consider her ways, and be wise: Which having no guide, overseer, or ruler, provideth her meat in the summer, and gathereth her food in the harvest. How long wilt thou sleep, O sluggard? when wilt thou arise out of thy sleep? Yet a little sleep, a little slumber, a little folding of the hands to sleep: So shall thy poverty come as one that travelleth, and thy want as an armed man. Proverbs 6:6-11

PERSONAL GOALS

Setting personal goals will:

➢ Give you energy and keep you moving forward
➢ Lessen stress
➢ Help you focus on important tasks
➢ Give you confidence
➢ Help you overcome barriers and obstacles
➢ Give purpose to your life

Without purpose, life has no meaning. Many people go through life aimlessly, doing the same thing every day and never making any changes. It's like wanting to take a trip somewhere, but not making any plans, so you don't really go anywhere.

It is OK if you set goals and don't reach them, but it is NOT OK if you don't try or even set any goals. Without goals in life, where are you going? God has a plan for each of us. Have you prayed and asked God to help you discover your goals?

Before setting goals, you need to understand that success is only possible if your goals are realistic and reachable. They need to have a specific purpose and be set within certain guidelines and timeframes.

Setting proper goals will give you a road map to success. We are going to show you how to **D.R.A.W.** your own personal roadmap with the following guidelines:

✓**D**efinite   ✓**R**ealistic   ✓**A**ssessable   ✓**W**ell-timed

On page 12 you were asked to write down your ultimate goal in life. What was this goal?

After going through this workbook, is your answer still the same? ☐ yes ☐no

If you have changed direction towards a new goal, what is it? _____

Why did you change your goal? _____

> For that ye ought to say, If the Lord will, we shall live, and do this, or that. James 4:15

D R.A.W. your goals - D efinite

Being definite about what you want to achieve will keep you focused and on track. If you aren't totally certain about what you want, it is easy to lose sight of where you are going.

Business people write business plans so they can have a clear picture of where they are going and see how it will lead them to success. People also need a personal business plan or goal plan to lead them to success.

Decide what your goals are, then:

> ➤ Write a clear step-by-step plan so you know exactly what you want to accomplish
> ➤ Start each day with determination
> ➤ Focus on your own thoughts and don't get sidetracked by what others say and do
> ➤ Even when you're disappointed or discouraged, it's important get going and take action.

On the following page there is a sample **DAILY PROMISE SHEET** on which you can create some daily goals. When you make a promise to yourself, you are more likely to keep your promise, so try to fill out this sheet every day and watch your progress as you try to improve on the day before. There is a blank template at the back of the book that you can use to make copies or create one of your own.

Remember to **be definite** in the goals you choose. Here are some examples of definite and not definite goals:

DEFINITE – I want to lose 50 lbs.   **NOT DEFINITE –** I would like to lose some weight.

DEFINITE – I am going to register for an accounting course tomorrow.   **NOT DEFINITE –** I am thinking about taking an accounting course.

DEFINITE – I am going to travel to Calgary in July.   **NOT DEFINITE –** I'm taking a trip this summer.

Think about 3 simple goals that you have. Write them in the spaces provided

1)

2)

3)

Are these goals definite or not definite? If they are non-definite, try to reword them to be definite.

MY DAILY PROMISE SHEET

1. Fill out the sheet every day. Mornings are best but anytime will work as long as you are consistent.
2. On the first day, you will leave column 1 and 2 empty.
3. Fill out columns 3-6 with "descriptive' words that explain how you feel for each area of your being. Don't use works like 'fine' or 'OK' as they don't require any thought. On the next page is a list of words that you can use.
4. In the last column, write down a daily commitment to improve in some area. This should be something that you can accomplish before the following day.
5. On the second and each consecutive day, check back on the Daily Promise you made and write down your progress and comments on the results.
6. At the end of the week, print out another sheet and continue working on it.
7. If you continue to keep your daily promise, you will probably notice that your state of well-being will positively change from week to week.

	PROGRESS FROM PROMISE	MY COMMENT ON PROMISE	MY PHYSICAL STATE	MY MENTAL STATE	MY EMOTIONAL STATE	MY SPIRITUAL STATE	MY DAILY PROMISE
M			Wounded Battered	Numb Confused	Depressed Scared Moody	Separated Weird	Call my counselor this morning for appointment
TU	Called and made appt with counselor	Felt good to talk to counselor and want to see her	Wounded Broken-up	Blaming Confused	Depressed Scared Moody	Separated Weird	Get out of bed, shower, dress and go to my appointment
W	Went to my appt –got some books to read	My counselor helped me with some problems – feel better	Un-comfortable Wounded	Blaming Thinking	Depressed Vulnerable	Separated	Contact a local support group about going to a weekly meeting
TH	Called the support group	Meetings are every Monday at 7pm	Wounded Un-comfortable	Blaming Open	Depressed Vulnerable	Separated	Start reading some books from my counselor
F	Read the first chapter of one book	Learned some valuable stuff	Wounded Un-comfortable	Blaming Open	Depressed Vulnerable	Separated	Read another chapter and go for a walk
SA	Read a chapter – walked for 30 min	Learned more stuff and walk helped me feel better	Wounded Un-comfortable	Open	Depressed	Separated	Read another chapter Go to church with a friend
SU	Read – went to church	Learned more – feel good	Wounded Calm	Open	Depressed	Open	Read Go to support group tomorrow

Commit your work to the Lord and your plans will be established – Proverbs 16:3

FEELING WORDS

Abandoned	Childlike	Friendly	Misunderstood	Shy
Abused	Cold	Frightened	Moody	Sincere
Accepted	Comfortable	Frustrated	Nasty	Smart
Accused	Comforted	Funny	Nervous	Sorry
Accepting	Complete	Generous	Numb	Special
Admired	Confident	Gentle	Obsessed	Strong
Adored	Confused	Genuine	Offended	Stubborn
Affectionate	Considerate	Giving	Open	Stupid
Agreeable	Content	Happy	Out of control	Successful
Aggressive	Courteous	Healthy	Overpowered	Surprised
Alive	Crazy	Helpful	Patient	Terrific
Alone	Creative	Helpless	Peaceful	Terrified
Amused	Critical	Hesitant	Pleasant	Tired
Angry	Criticized	Honest	Pleased	Tolerant
Annoyed	Crushed	Honoured	Positive	Tormented
Anxious	Curious	Hopeful	Powerful	Torn
Apologetic	Dangerous	Hopeless	Powerless	Touchy
Appreciated	Dead	Humiliated	Pressured	Trusted
Appreciative	Deceived	Hurt	Pretending	Trustful
Apprehensive	Defensive	Ignorant	Pretty	Trusting
Argumentative	Delighted	Ignored	Proud	Ugly
Astonished	Dependent	Impatient	Put down	Unacceptable
Assertive	Depressed	Important	Puzzled	Uncertain
Attacked	Dirty	Incompetent	Quiet	Uncomfortable
Attractive	Disgusted	Incomplete	Real	Under control
Aware	Distressed	Independent	Regretful	Understanding
Battered	Distrustful	Insecure	Rejected	Understood
Beautiful	Disturbed	Innocent	Relaxed	Unhappy
Belittled	Doubtful	Insignificant	Resentful	Unsafe
Bereaved	Eager	Inspired	Responsible	Upset
Betrayed	Embarrassed	Insulted	Respected	Useful
Blamed	Empowered	Interested	Restless	Useless
Blaming	Empty	Irrational	Safe	Unworthy
Bored	Enraged	Irresponsible	Satisfied	Valuable
Brave	Enthusiastic	Irritable	Scared	Valued
Calm	Excited	Irritated	Secure	Violated
Capable	Fake	Isolated	Self-conscious	Violent
Careful	Foolish	Jealous	Selfish	Vulnerable
Caring	Forced	Judging	Separated	Weak
Cautious	Forceful	Lonely	Sensuous	Whole
Certain	Forgiven	Loving	Serious	Willing
Cheated	Forgotten	Lucky	Shattered	Withdrawn
Cheerful	Free	Miserable	Shocked	Worried

D. R A.W. your goals - R ealistic

Be Realistic when setting goals. You have to be able to achieve what you want to do and this requires an honest look at what you can physically, mentally and emotionally accomplish. It is always good to stretch your abilities or 'reach for the stars', but you also have to make sure that your goals are not way beyond your capabilities.

We often look at what other people are accomplishing and then try to set our personal goals to meet their standards instead of our own. Make sure you aren't trying to do something that is another person's idea or something you have convinced yourself is real.

Set your goals without putting too much emphasis on your environment, your financial situation, where you live or where you work. These things should definitely be taken into consideration, but your situation can change when you start working towards your goals and you become more confident.

Then we also have to be careful that we don't set our goals too low either. We may be afraid to try anything because we fear rejection and failure. Don't settle for second best because you think you aren't capable of doing something. Set goals high enough so you have to reach and stretch, but not so high that you are overwhelmed and can't manage them. Pray for guidance. It requires a lot of hard work and patience, but if you stay positive and keep working on your goals, it will help your confidence grow.

Would the following goals be realistic? Circle yes or no and write a short explanation for your answer.

Check our answers at the back of the book.

1) A 40 year old lady wants to take ballet classes. Yes No

2) A 30 year old man is almost blind and wants to race cars. Yes No

3) A 50 year old lady wants to be a doctor, but never graduated from high school. Yes No

4) A 30 year old man wants to teach piano lessons but he has never played piano before. Yes No

5) A 20 year old lady wants to open a clothing store, but has no money. Yes No

6) A 40 year old man registers for a 5 year course and tells everyone he will graduate in 2 years. Yes No

The best way to set goals is to break larger goals into smaller goals that you can reach as you journey along. If you think you can reach your goals, you just might do so. But if you think you can't and don't even try, you certainly won't.

It helps to get some positive support in place to help you reach your goals. This could be a family member, friend, organization or support group. There are numerous possibilities.

Some people may prefer to keep some goals as personal and not share them with anyone else. This is fine, but keep in mind that you may be helping others by sharing your goals with them. It will give them an opportunity to help you and it may even encourage them to set and work on their own goals. Working with others will also help you reach your goals quicker.

Who do you think would be helpful to you in reaching your goals?
Think of a least 3 family members or friends. Make sure these are people that you can trust to help and support you. If you can't think of anyone, check out your local groups and organizations. There are many helpful volunteers who would be happy to work with you. Look in the yellow pages or check on the internet. Write down the names and phone numbers below:

1) _____

2) _____

3) _____

It can be helpful to create a visual image of your goals so you can look at them and see how realistic they are. In the space below, try to draw a simple picture of your goals. Then spend a few minutes trying to decide if they look realistic to you.

And Jesus said unto them, Because of your unbelief: for verily I say unto you, If ye have faith as a grain of mustard seed, ye shall say unto this mountain, Remove hence to yonder place; and it shall remove; and nothing shall be impossible unto you.
Matthew 17:20

D.R.⬛A⬛W. your goals - ⬛A⬛ssessable

Goals need to be Assessable. There needs to be a way to assess or measure your success in what you are doing, so you know if you are making progress. Revisit your goals regularly to keep focused. Analyze them, update them, make changes and anticipate problems. Then celebrate your successes.

How will your goals affect your life? Will they make an impact?

Here are some questions that will help you evaluate the effectiveness of your goals:

1) <u>What have I learned</u>? This refers to any gained knowledge, new skills and any mistakes to avoid next time.
2) <u>What actions have worked or not worked</u>? List the details of how specific tasks have been effective.
3) <u>Did my smaller goals and tasks support the larger goal</u>? Give details of any actions that didn't provide the expected results.
4) <u>What progress has been made</u>? In each of the categories, state if you have made any progress and explain how you have grown emotionally, physically, intellectually, and spiritually.
5) <u>Have my relationships with others improved</u>? Give details of any improvements or where any problems have resulted.
6) <u>Do I need to make any adjustments to my short-term goals</u>? Explain any changes that need to be done in order to reach your goals.
7) <u>Is there anything missing from my goal plan</u>? Explain what should be added.

It is critical that these questions be asked on a regular basis in order to monitor the success of your plan. Start by doing this every week or two for the first couple of months, then you could start doing it once a month. You could also ask your family and friends if they see any changes.

If you have reached your goal, you should give yourself a reward. This will help reinforce newly created good habits and give you a personal incentive to keep moving forward.

Some ideas for rewarding yourself could be:

➤ A SMALL portion of a special treat (ice cream, cake, chocolate)
➤ A new outfit
➤ A bubble bath
➤ Renting a movie
➤ Going for coffee with a friend

What would your special rewards be? _____

_____

> Delight thyself also in the LORD: and he shall give thee the desires of thine heart. Commit thy way unto the LORD; trust also in him; and he shall bring it to pass. Psalm 37:4-5

D.R.A.W your goals - Well-timed

Set goals that are well-timed. Certain things can be done during certain times of your life according to your age and capabilities. For each goal, you need to specify a starting time and a deadline. Make sure the time frame matches the difficulty of the goal and then monitor your success. Steady progress with positive results will help build confidence and increase esteem.

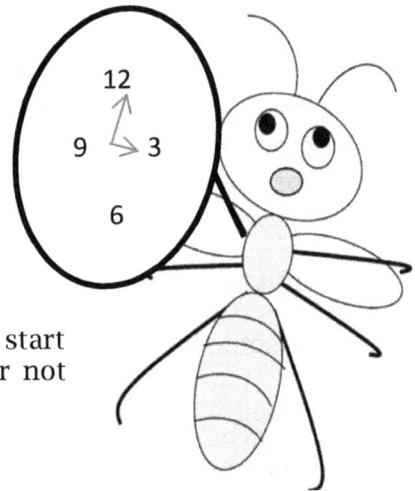

When you set goals, it is important to get going and start accomplishing things. Time can be a huge factor in whether or not you will be successful. You will lose a lot of precious time if you:

- Procrastinate
- Put things aside
- Don't finish them
- Don't even start them
- Are too cautious
- Too careless

How do you use or plan your time? Time is always a problem – there are never enough hours in a day for some people – for others there is too much time. We need to use our time effectively by planning and making goals.

Using a journal to track your time is a good idea. This will help you manage your life, instead of life managing you. Write down what you do in 30 minute increments and then at the end of each week, take a look at what you have written and determine what time you have wasted (watching TV, talking on the phone, playing on the computer, sleeping, other).

Here are 5 ways to conquer procrastination:

1) **Spend time in prayer** - Ask God to help guide you in fulfilling His plans for you.

2) **Get organized** - If you are prepared for each day with specific plans, you will limit the chance of procrastination and start forming good habits.

3) **Break down tasks** – Take your large goals and break them down into smaller goals. Working on bite-sized tasks will help make your larger goals more realistic and easier to achieve.

4) **Tell others** - If you tell people that you are working on certain goals, it adds healthy pressure that will push you forward when you experience any weak moments.

5) **Challenge yourself** – Look at procrastination as 'the enemy' that is trying to convince you to stop working on your plans. Tell yourself that you will overcome any influence it may have on your life and keep moving forward to achieve your goals.

Commitment is imperative when creating a goal plan but also when following through on your plans.

> Whereas ye know not what shall be on the morrow. For what is your life? It is even a vapour, that appeareth for a little time, and then vanisheth away. James 4:14

YOU WILL FAIL

REMEMBER THAT WE ARE HUMAN AND WE ALL MAKE MISTAKES – SO DON'T BE SURPRISED WHEN THIS HAPPENS.

When you start working on your goals, you **WILL** have some setbacks or even failures, but this is a normal part of life and can be an excellent learning process. Failures can motivate us to work harder towards our goals and make necessary changes.

Just remember to keep going and if you don't give up, you WILL have some rewards. **WE ARE OUR OWN WORST ENEMIES** and we take better care of others than we do ourselves. We need to care for our own health, eat properly, exercise and sleep enough.

NEVER, NEVER GIVE UP!! Life will always test us and it is up to us whether or not we succeed. Nobody else can succeed for us and we need to learn how to fail successfully.

If you miss a deadline for reaching a goal, ask yourself why you missed it.
- Was it too hard to reach?
- Where you slack in working towards it?
- Did 'life' get in the way?
- Did you ask God to help you?

You need to put things in proper perspective. Remember that every time we move ahead 2 steps, we might be thrown backwards a step or two. Rework your goals and then start moving ahead again. Missed goals will slow you down for a bit, but it won't erase all the work you have already done. Having a failure won't keep you from reaching your long term goals as long as you keep working on them.

When you do fail, what action do you take? Do you blame others, give up, make excuses like:
- It's just too hard
- I can't succeed
- I grew up in an abusive home
- I didn't go to college
- It's God's fault
- The government doesn't help people like me
- My boss holds me back
- I don't have the time or money

What is one failure in your life that you can remember? _____

_____

How did you react to this failure? _____

_____

Did you learn something from this failure? _____

_____

> **For in many things we offend all. If any man offend not in word, the same is a perfect man, and able also to bridle the whole body. James 3:2**

IF YOU'VE NEVER FAILED, YOU'VE NEVER LIVED

Everyone has had their share of difficulty in life, some worse than others, but the successful ones just get up and keep trying. Most successful people have failed many times, but never stop moving towards their goals. We need to be responsible for ourselves and be strong.

> I can do all things through Christ which strengtheneth me. Philippians 4:13

If you have failed, you are in good company. Here are some famous people who failed in their personal lives. You will probably recognize some of the names.

- ➤ **LUCILLE BALL** failed at the drama school she attended. They said she was too shy and it would be a waste of their time to teach her. She went on to become a famous actress.
- ➤ **THE BEATLES** failed when the Decca recording company wouldn't accept their music because it was no longer popular. The Beatles soon became famous recording artists.
- ➤ **BEETHOVEN** failed when his music teacher said he would never make it as a composer. Beethoven became very famous, continuing to write even after becoming deaf.
- ➤ **WINSTON CHURCHILL** failed the sixth grade and was defeated in several elections until he became Prime Minister in England.
- ➤ **ULYSSES S GRANT** failed as a soldier, farmer and real estate agent, then at the age of 38 he became a handyman for his own father. Later he became the 18th President of the United States.
- ➤ **WALT DISNEY** failed at his newspaper job because they told him he did not have any original ideas or a good imagination. His lack of imagination created Disneyland.
- ➤ **EINSTEIN** failed in his parents' eyes as they thought he was intellectually challenged. He developed the Theory of Relativity and later received a Nobel Prize in Physics.
- ➤ **ABRAHAM LINCOLN** failed twice in business, was defeated in 8 elections and after his fiancé died, he had a nervous breakdown. Later he became the 16th President of the United States.
- ➤ **HENRY FORD** failed in the first 2 companies he started, then founded the Ford Motor Company.
- ➤ **THOMAS EDISON** failed at school. His teacher thought he was too stupid to learn and told him he would only be successful at a job using his pleasant personality. Later he developed the phonograph, the motion picture camera and the light bulb.

THESE PEOPLE ALL FAILED BEFORE THEY WERE SUCCESSFUL!!! The key to their success was having confidence in their abilities, not listening to what others said about them and not giving up on their goals in life.

Failure isn't a problem in life unless you dwell on it and stop growing. Learn from your failures and try not to make the same mistake again. There is a lesson to be learned in everything we do in life.

If you never failed, you would never learn how to deal with difficulty in life. Failures can destroy you or make you stronger – it is all how you react in these situations. Treat failures as stepping stones to future successes.

Achieving your goals will not be easy. It requires hard work even when things get tough and a lot of patience when you have setbacks or experience failures. Always remember that you must keep going in order to succeed.

ROAD BLOCKS

The first thing you have to decide is what you want out of life. Everyone has different needs and desires, so our goals will all be different. There are certain guidelines to follow, but each of us will follow a different path to reach our goal.

Before you get started on setting some goals, you need to determine if there is anything blocking you or holding you back.

Many times, fear holds people back from pursuing their goals in life. Others are too busy filling the needs of others (family, friends, co-workers) and use this as an excuse for not being able to make any changes in their lives. Even bad habits may be holding us back. It is necessary to eliminate any of these blocks before you will be able to move forward and reach your goals. Pray and ask God to reveal any blocks that may be in your way.

What interests and abilities do you have? These can be things that you are doing now, things you have done, or things you have never done.

If you ask a child what they want to be when they grow up, they will say, "a lawyer, fireman, teacher, astronaut, president, and so on. By the time the adult emerges, these dreams are often forgotten. These dreams need to be revisited while thinking about things you have done and maybe are doing right now, that you might like to pursue.

Write down 3 things that would make you happy today.

1)

2)

3)

If it were possible to do these things right now, would they still be making you happy in a month? ☐ yes ☐ no ☐ maybe

If it were possible to do these things right now, would they still be making you happy next year?   ☐ yes ☐ no ☐ maybe

Sometimes we want things to happen immediately, yet often these same things aren't even important after a period of time passes. We may want to take an expensive vacation right now, but if we have borrowed money, it may not still be making us happy two years from now when we are struggling to make payments.

In setting goals, we need to consider what we need in the future and not just the present. Everything we do has consequences and we should take the time to think things through carefully.

> **Be ye strong therefore, and let not your hands be weak: for your work shall be rewarded. 1 Chronicles 15:7**

SETTING YOUR GOALS

Goals may include topics of health, work, education, money and relationships. Here are some common goals:

1. Losing weight
2. Becoming debt-free
3. Getting a diploma
4. Going back to school
5. Making new friends
6. Getting a better job
7. Writing a book
8. Dealing with anger
9. Making more money
10. Taking a vacation

Each person will have their own ideas and dreams and will have to determine what are most important to them in their own lives. We may have several topics of interest, but we need to make sure we choose the most important and work on those goals.

In determining which goals are most important, you can use a simple worksheet. Following is a list of 9 different topics numbered 1-10. Put a check under the appropriate number. (1 is least important and 10 extremely important).

	1	2	3	4	5	6	7	8	9	10
My family										
My friends										
My job/career										
My education										
My health										
My relationships										
My money										
My spiritual life										
My recreation										

Ideally, you should have just 1 topic checked in each column. If you have more than just one, it may be necessary for you to go back and think carefully about which are more important than others and change your answers. You can certainly work on more than 1 goal at a time, but it is easier if you work on one topic with 1 ultimate goal that is broken down into several smaller goals. This could be a learning goal, a career goal or a behavior goal. Once you have achieved that goal, you can start working on another goal.

YOUR ULTIMATE GOAL

It's time to get ready and set your goals. Start by getting organized in a comfortable, quiet location. Take a pad of paper, a pen and your journal if you have one. Then gather your thoughts and start writing. Don't forget to ask God to help guide your thoughts.

On page 57, we asked you to revise your goal from page 12. What was that new goal?

Think about your answer. Is this something that you can't live without? Is this what you have always been dreaming about? If this is the only option you want, then you should working towards it. If not, you might need to change direction as you go, but start working on something. You can always make changes as you go along.

Is your goal realistic? Do you have the skills or talents necessary to accomplish the goal or can

you learn them? ---

Do you think you can accomplish your goal and why? ------------------------------------

----

What is the first step necessary to reach that goal and what date are you going to take that first step?

How will you measure your progress and how often? ------------------------------------

----

Have you overcome any road blocks that may stop you from reaching your goal or do you need

to work on removing any? ---

What date would you like to reach your Ultimate Goal? ---------------------------------

> **A man's heart deviseth his way: but the LORD directeth his steps.**
> **Proverbs 16:9**

A SAMPLE GOAL

Here are three possible ultimate goals, broken down with smaller goals.

1) ULTIMATE GOAL - LOSING 100 POUNDS
   - smaller goals could include daily exercise, preparing healthy menus and creating a daily schedule
2) ULTIMATE GOAL - BECOMING DEBT-FREE
   - smaller goals could include a monthly budget plan, opening a savings account, paying cash for certain items instead of charging them
3) ULTIMATE GOAL - GETTING AN ACCOUNTING DIPLOMA
   - smaller goals could include planning time for study and work, getting financial assistance and budgeting expenses

Let's do a quick personal goal review. Please answer the following questions.

What are you doing right now?	
What would you like to be doing in 1 month?	
What would you like to be doing in 6 months?	
What would you like to be doing in 1 year?	
What would you like to be doing in 5 years?	
What would you like to be doing in 10 years?	
What is my long term goal?	

Below is a sample goal sheet for <u>Ultimate Goal #1 – Losing 100 pounds.</u>

MY ULTIMATE GOAL – TO LOSE 100 POUNDS IN 2 YEARS AND LOWER MY BLOOD PRESSURE

D.efinite	Why do you want to reach this goal?	Because I am overweight and having some health issues
	Who is going to be involved?	God, myself, family, friends
	What do you want to accomplish?	Lose weight and reduce blood pressure
	How will you work on your goal?	Walking, biking, exercising
	Where will you work on goal?	On the street, at the gym
R.ealistic	Is your goal physically possible?	Yes, my health is good enough to manage this
	Is your goal mentally possible?	Yes, I have learned the best ways to lose weight
	Is your goal emotionally possible?	Yes, I have support from family and friends
	Are there any road blocks to remove?	No, I am no longer afraid of looking stupid and can face others.
	Is this your goal or someone else's?	This is my goal
A.ssessable	How much or how many?	100 pounds, 2 per week
	How can I measure this?	Charts, journal, clothing size, scales, doctor visits
W.ell-timed	When will you start working on your goal?	March 1, 2011
	When will you complete your goal?	March 1, 2013

SMALLER GOALS

DAILY	Walk for 30 minutes	9 am
2X WEEK	Go for a bike ride for 30 min	Wed and Sat at 1pm
WEEKLY	Exercise at the gym for 1 hr	Friday at 7pm
WEEKLY	Monitor weight with scales	Monday at 7 am
DAILY	Eat healthy foods/cut portion sizes	Reduce fats, carbs and eliminate sugar
DAILY	Write progress in journal	Mark weight on calendar – goal of 2 lbs/wk
DAILY	Pray, read scripture	8 am

REWARDS FOR REACHING GOALS

Weekly check on weight – go for coffee with friends
Keeping regular exercise routine for month – take spouse to a movie
Keeping proper diet for a month – take family to lunch at a healthy restaurant
Losing 100 pounds in 2 years– take family on a camping trip to the Rocky Mountains

NOW IT'S YOUR TURN TO MAKE SOME GOALS. Use the following template or create one of your own. There is also a blank template at the back of the book if you need more copies. Mark your checkpoints on a calendar to keep track of your progress. When you reach your goals, make sure to reward yourself for a job well done!

MY ULTIMATE GOAL –		
D.efinite	Why do you want to reach this goal?	
	Who is going to be involved in this goal?	
	What do you want to accomplish?	
	How will you work on your goal?	
	Where will you work on your goal?	
R.ealistic	Is your goal physically possible?	
	Is your goal mentally possible?	
	Is your goal emotionally possible?	
	Are there any road blocks to remove?	
	Is this your goal or someone else's?	
A.ssessable	How much or how many?	
	How can I measure this?	
W.ell-timed	When will you start working on your goal?	
	When will you complete your goal?	

SMALLER GOALS

REWARDS FOR REACHING GOALS

In all thy ways acknowledge him, and he shall direct thy paths.
Proverbs 3:6

Goals will always have a beginning but may not always have an end. Goals can have specific deadlines or they can be ongoing. Even if your goals have deadlines, they can be renewed. For example if you had the goal of losing 100 pounds in 2 year, you may certainly reach that goal. However, you might still be overweight by 20 pounds and you can extend the deadline or set another goal to lose that weight.

Certain goals that pertain to improving attitudes and building character should be ongoing. They will help increase confidence and create strong esteem. These goals can be tracked in a daily journal so you can see if you are making progress. Reviewing your journal on a regular basis will keep you motivated and on-track.

Examples of ongoing goals:

- To be thankful to God
- To be loving and kind
- To be considerate
- To be caring and compassionate
- To be patient
- To be a good example to others
- To be generous
- To be understanding
- To be honest and trustworthy
- To spend quality time with family and friends
- To always do the best possible in every situation

We become the person we think we are, not always the person we want to become. We put ourselves in a box that is created by society, one that is controlled by other people or things (work, possessions, addictions). Then we stay in that box because we feel safe. It is easier than trying to break free from our captivity and face unknown fears.

Set goals to get out of your box and work hard at keeping those goals. Make the choice to live the life that you dream about. Stop pretending that you are in control of your life and be honest with yourself. Are you really in control or who/what is? Are you living in a box? Why do you stay there?

Now is the time to make a change. Take action and start controlling your own life. **You are the only one who can make choices for yourself, so make the right ones.**

Don't wait any longer. Start today. What is stopping you?

> **But seek ye first the kingdom of God, and his righteousness; and all these things shall be added unto you. Take therefore no thought for the morrow: for the morrow shall take thought for the things of itself. Sufficient unto the day is the evil thereof. Matthew 6:33-34**

IN CONCLUSION

If you have completed this workbook, I would like to congratulate you on the hard work you have done. Give yourself a pat on the back and tell yourself how proud you are for a job well done. It isn't easy to look at yourself with honesty and determine where your strengths and weaknesses lie. This takes real courage but it will build a beautiful character!

You have now begun your journey to happiness and success. If you keep focused on the goals you have set and continue moving forward, you should notice positive changes in your life. The most important goal for you should be to put God first in your life and then everything else will start to come together. Some changes will happen quickly, others may take time, so be patient and don't give up easily when things don't happen as quickly as you had planned. We have to remember that God is in control and His timing is not our timing. He may hold us back for His purposes or take His time in order so we can learn and grow closer to Him.

Always try to surround yourself with positive people who will lift you up and help support and encourage you. Make sure you do the same to other people, showing love and kindness to everyone. Also try to go places and do things that make you feel positive about yourself. You should always avoid going anywhere that makes you feel bad or do anything that you know is not good for you. It is often easier to stick with old habits and do the wrong thing than to step out of your comfort zone and try something new.

It is also a good idea to review this workbook once in a while to remind you about what you have learned and keep you focused on being positive. Remember that YOU DO have self-control and YOU CAN make your own choices. Choose wisely even when things are hard and you will soon find your life getting easier, one step at a time. Work on today and do the best you can. Then tomorrow, work on today again and keep going. God loves you and He will help you reach your goals!

- ➢ **Be committed to moving ahead**
- ➢ **Make some positive changes**
- ➢ **Stay focused**
- ➢ **Never, never, never give up** and you will find the success and happiness you have been searching for.

If this workbook has helped you, we would appreciate hearing your story. Please send an email to imconfident@live.ca with your comments. If you are interested in having your story or comments posted on our website (first name and last initial only), please provide authorization in your email. Otherwise we will use it for information purposes only. Thank-you.

PLEASE VISIT OUR WEBSITE FOR INFORMATION, ARTICLES, UPDATES, ACTIVITIES AND MORE.......

www.imconfident.com

ANSWER PAGE

Answers to page 30 – Positive Things

Hugs, saying thanks, reading stories, encouraging words, helping clean room, smiles, going to the park, sharing toys, giving a gift.

Answers to page 36 – Positive and Negative Fuel

1Neg	2Neg	3Pos	4Neg	5Neg	6Pos	7Pos	8Neg	9Neg	10Pos
11Pos	12Neg	13Pos	14Pos	15Pos	16Pos	17Pos	18Neg	19Pos	

Answers to page 47 – Hygiene Quizzes

1) YES - Every time you use a washroom, you touch things with bacteria that can cause sickness.

2) YES - Use your own personal soap to avoid picking up someone else's germs.

3) YES - When a toilet flushes, a fine bacteria-spray goes out several feet into the room where it lands on everything. This spray cannot be seen by the naked eye.

4) YES - Carry something to wipe your nose when it runs and to stop sneezes that spread germs.

5) YES - Hand sanitizer stops germs and is handy when you don't have access to water and soap.

6) YES - It is important to stop offensive body odour - it can affect relationships and work.

7) NO - Animals lick many things that may have bacteria or germs.

8) NO - If you are comfortable eating the food, you should be comfortable using the utensils.

9) NO - Never share personal items.

10) NO - Never share personal items.

11) NO - Never pick up food off the floor as it could have germs, dust or hair.

12) and 13) NO - Never share personal items as it could spread germs and cause skin conditions.

1) Dental checkups should be twice annually for maximum benefits. If cost is an issue, at least once a year is advisable.

2) You should shower or bathe at least once daily - more often if involved in strenuous activities or dirty work.

3) Teeth should be brushed when you get up, after every meal and before going to bed.

4) Sheets should be washed weekly or at least twice a month depending on how much you sweat.

Wash your hands often and thoroughly, especially at these times:

    *before eating   *after touching animal   *after eating   *when preparing food

    *before and after visiting a sick friend   *after taking out the garbage   *after cleaning the toilet

Answers to page 61 – Realistic goals

1) YES - if she wants to learn ballet for fun and she is in good physical condition

   NO - if she wants to become a professional ballet dancer. Most retire by age 35 or 40 and a proper ballet school would not accept a 40 yr old as it requires a young body and years of practice to learn ballet and perform properly.

2) NO - It would be impossible to drive without sight, unless the condition can be surgically repaired.

3) YES - If she is mentally and physically capable of learning to be a doctor, she could go to school and learn. It would require a huge commitment and a lot of hard work.

4) YES - It is possible, but would require years of practice and a total commitment to working hard.

5) YES - It is possible if she has good credit and can get a small loan to get started, or even borrow money from family members.

6) NO - It is not possible to complete a 5 year course in 2 years.

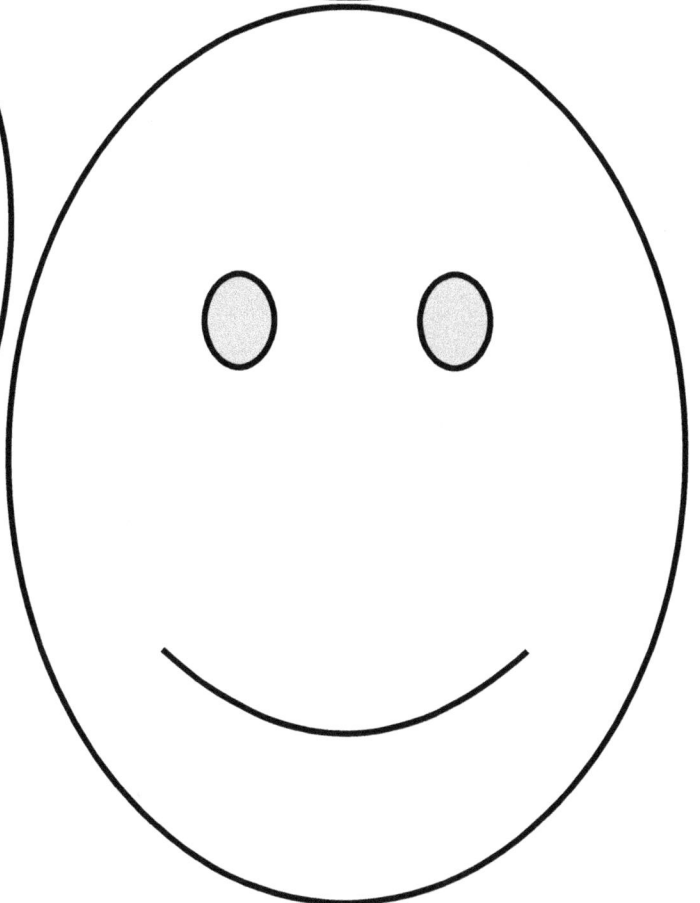

My Daily Promise Sheet for _____

	PROGRESS FROM PROMISE	MY COMMENT ON PROMISE	MY PHYSICAL STATE	MY MENTAL STATE	MY EMOTIONAL STATE	MY SPIRITUAL STATE	MY DAILY PROMISE
M							
TU							
W							
TH							
F							
SA							
SU							

NOTES

BIBLE VERSE STUDY

GENESIS 1:27 So God created man in His own image, in the image of God created He him; male and female created He them. Mankind was created to resemble God in certain ways and we were placed on earth as men and women to represent the Creator. If we are created in God's image, we should be proud of ourselves and our bodies.

GENESIS 2:8 And the LORD God planted a garden eastward in Eden; and there He put the man whom He had formed. God wanted His creation to live in a beautiful garden. He did this because we are special in His eyes and He loves us.

GENESIS 9:3 Every moving thing that liveth shall be meat for you; even as the green herb have I given you all things. When mankind was created, they were vegetarians. After the flood, people were permitted to eat meat. God wants us to have sufficient food to eat, so He provided well for us.

JOSHUA 1:8 This book of the law shall not depart out of thy mouth; but thou shalt meditate therein day and night. We are supposed to meditate on God's word and fill our hearts and minds with it continuously so it will give us daily strength.

1 SAMUEL 16:7 But the LORD said to Samuel, "Do not look on his appearance or on the height of his stature, because I have rejected him. For the LORD sees not as man sees: man looks on the outward appearance, but the LORD looks on the heart." Our outward appearance is not nearly as important as our inward appearance. Society today encourages us to judge others by how they look and dress. God sees our heart and judges our inner appearance.

1 CHRONICLES 15:7 Be ye strong therefore, and let not your hands be weak: for your work shall be rewarded. God has given us the strength to do many things. We are to keep busy doing good work and not allow our hands to be idle, so God can reward us.

PSALMS 19:14 Let the words of my mouth, and the meditation of my heart, be acceptable in Thy sight, O LORD, my strength, and my redeemer. Words are very powerful and they can help people or hurt people. We should always try to ensure that the words we speak and the feelings we have in our hearts will be acceptable to God.

PSALMS 22:19 But be not thou far from me, O LORD: O my strength, haste thee to help me. When we are in trouble and need help, we often turn to other people or try to figure things out ourselves which just gets us in more trouble. The first thing we should do is ask God to help us and give us strength.

PSALM 37:4-5 Delight thyself also in the LORD: and he shall give thee the desires of thine heart. Commit thy way unto the LORD; trust also in him; and he shall bring it to pass. Many times when we are trying to do something that we feel God has been leading us to do, we hit road blocks and don't seem to be getting anywhere. We need to trust in Him and commit ourselves to keep going, knowing that He is there for us and will help us on our journey.

PSALM 63:1 O God, thou art my God; early will I seek Thee: my soul thirsteth for Thee, my flesh longeth for Thee in a dry and thirsty land, where no water is, We live in a world that is like a huge wasteland or desert and sometimes we feel thirsty and there is nothing around us that refreshes us like a cool drink of water. If we seek God, He can quench our thirst and refresh our souls.

PSALM 118:8 It is better to trust in the LORD than to put confidence in man. If we trust people to help us with our problems, we will be disappointed. We need to trust in God and ask Him to help us.

PSALM 139:14 I will praise thee; for I am fearfully and wonderfully made: marvellous are thy works; and that my soul knoweth right well. Many people don't believe they have value and feel bad about themselves. Society continually finds fault with us and makes us feel worthless. The truth is, God created us and loves every part of us. God doesn't create junk and we should praise Him for creating such a magnificent work of art.

PROVERBS 3:6 In all thy ways acknowledge him, and he shall direct thy paths. We have to turn every area of our lives over to God and allow Him to guide us along the pathway that He has chosen for us.

PROVERBS 3:24 When thou liest down, thou shalt not be afraid: yea, thou shalt lie down, and thy sleep shall be sweet. Getting a good night's sleep is important to our health. When we go to bed, we should pray and ask God to bring us peace so we can sleep securely and with no fear.

PROVERBS 6:6-11 Go to the ant, thou sluggard; consider her ways, and be wise: Which having no guide, overseer, or ruler, provideth her meat in the summer, and gathereth her food in the harvest. How long wilt thou sleep, O sluggard? when wilt thou arise out of thy sleep? Yet a little sleep, a little slumber, a little folding of the hands to sleep: So shall thy poverty come as one that travelleth, and thy want as an armed man. These verses talk about procrastination and wanting to put off doing things that may result in not achieving success in our lives. We should pay attention to the tiny ant who is a diligent and hard worker. It gets a lot accomplished without having anyone supervising its work. It focuses on getting the work done so it will be well provided for.

PROVERBS 16:3 Commit thy works to the Lord and thy thoughts shall be established. The best way to ensure that our dreams and goals will be achieved is to ask God to help us on our journey. When we go to Him for help, He will work in us and through us to complete our task.

PROVERBS 16:9 A man's heart deviseth his way: but the LORD directeth his steps. We can spend a lot of time planning our future, but we have to understand that God alone will ensure that our plans ever come to pass. We need to always include Him in any plans we make.

PROVERBS 16:24 Pleasant words are as a honeycomb, sweet to the soul, and health to the bones. We should always try to use our words to help people. Positive words can lift people up, support and encourage them. Negative words can tear people down and discourage them. Pleasant words can be medicine for the soul.

PROVERBS 22:6 Train up a child in the way he should go; even when he is old he will not depart from it. Raising a child is difficult but if you give them a solid foundation when they are young, they will develop good habits that are hard to break. Children should be taught about God and how to tell right from wrong. Children are born sinners and if they are allowed to follow their own wishes, they will not be prepared for their adult life.

PROVERBS 23:20-21 Be not among winebibbers; among riotous eaters of flesh: For the drunkard and the glutton shall come to poverty: We have to be careful who we surround ourselves with or we may be influenced in a negative way. If we are with people who are addicted to eating or drinking too much, we may very well go the same way and it will ruin our health.

PROVERBS 31:30 Favour is deceitful, and beauty is vain, but a woman that feareth the LORD, she shall be praised. It is not good when women are vain or conceited about their outward beauty. Beauty fades and does not show the true character of a person. Women who have noble character and fear the Lord have much to be praised for.

ECCLESIASTES 3:13 And also that every man should eat and drink, and enjoy the good of all his labour, it is the gift of God. God wants all His children to enjoy life. His gift to us is that we have enough to eat and drink and to enjoy all the things he has worked hard for. Everything in our lives should not be done to extremes but have good balance.

ISAIAH 64:8 But now, O LORD, thou art our Father; we are the clay, and thou our potter; and we all are the work of Thy hand. God created us to be the person we are and only He can make changes for us. We have to ask Him to help us make positive changes in our lives.

JEREMIAH 26:13 Therefore now amend your ways and your doings, and obey the voice of the LORD your God; and the LORD will repent him of the evil that he hath pronounced against you. God wants us to repent of our sins, change our evil ways and listen to His voice.

MATTHEW 6:33-34 But seek ye first the kingdom of God, and his righteousness; and all these things shall be added unto you. Take therefore no thought for the morrow: for the morrow shall take thought for the things of itself. Sufficient unto the day is the evil thereof. When we put God first in our lives, he will guarantee our future needs. We are to put our trust in God and not worry about tomorrow. God has everything under control. It is enough for us to take care of today's needs.

MATTHEW 17:20 And Jesus said unto them, Because of your unbelief: for verily I say unto you, If ye have faith as a grain of mustard seed, ye shall say unto this mountain, Remove hence to yonder place; and it shall remove; and nothing shall be impossible unto you. God is telling us that we need to have faith and believe that nothing is impossible for Him. If it is in His plan, He will remove any obstacles in our way. We have to take Him seriously.

MARK 12:30-31 And thou shalt love the Lord thy God with all thy heart, and with all thy soul, and with all thy mind, and with all thy strength: this is the first commandment. And the second is like, namely this, Thou shalt love thy neighbour as thyself. There is none other commandment greater than these. The most important thing we can do is love God more than anything else. Then we are to love others the same way that we love ourselves. We are to love God more than ourselves and love others as ourselves. Material things are not even mentioned because only God and people are important.

LUKE 12:7 But even the very hairs of your head are all numbered. Fear not therefore: ye are of more value than many sparrows. The value of sparrows is very little. In Bible days, 2 sparrows were sold for a mere copper coin. Yet God loves every living creature in the world, even the sparrows. He reminds us in this verse how much more valuable we are than many sparrows. He loves us so much that he even knows how many hairs are on our heads!

JOHN 3:16 For God so loved the world, that He gave His only begotten Son, that whosoever believeth in Him should not perish but have everlasting life. This is probably the most well-known verse in the Bible. It summarizes in just a few words, the entire gospel, making His love very clear. God does not love our sins or the wicked ways of the world, but He loves all His children and doesn't want any of us to perish. He sent His Son into the world to save us. All we have to do is acknowledge Jesus Christ as our personal Saviour. Once we receive what Christ has done for us, God will give us eternal life.

JOHN 4:14 But whosoever drinketh of the water that I shall give him shall never thirst; but the water that I shall give him shall be in him a well of water springing up into everlasting life. We all need water to survive but just drinking the water from this world will never satisfy our thirst completely. The water that Jesus gives us, His blessings and mercies, will satisfy us in this world and in eternity as well.

JOHN 7:24 Judge not according to the appearance, but judge righteous judgment. The Jewish people in Bible times judged the outer appearance and didn't look at the inside of a person. They judged by sight and not by reality. This is not the right way to judge people. We need to look into their heart and see what is really going on.

JOHN 15:2 Every branch in me that beareth not fruit He taketh away: and every branch that beareth fruit, He purgeth it, that it may bring forth more fruit. Jesus is the true vine and we are the branches. In order to grow and bear fruit, the branches need to draw their life and nourishment from the vine. It is also necessary to prune back the branches so they will become stronger. We can bear fruit by spending time in prayer, reading scripture, being in fellowship with other believers and staying consciously connected with God. If we are not bearing any fruit, we will be separated from God and not receive His blessings. If we are bearing fruit, God will 'prune' us back from anything worldly that is holding us back from receiving all He wants us to have.

JOHN 15:9 As the Father hath loved me, so have I loved you: continue ye in my love. The love that God has for us is the same love that He has for His Son. His love is a great, unmeasurable love that can never be totally understood by man. We have to keep reminding ourselves how much God loves us and learn to enjoy our lives.

ROMANS 12:2 And be not conformed to this world: but be ye transformed by the renewing of your mind, that ye may prove what is that good, and acceptable, and perfect, will of God. We are warned not to let the world trap us into following their wicked lifestyles. Satan rules the world and tries to attract and capture us with temptations. When we are saved, we live in the world but we are not of the world. Christ died to deliver us and we are to testify that salvation is available to anyone who puts their trust in God. We have to separate ourselves from the world and keep renewing our minds daily by trying to think the way God thinks.

1 CORINTHIANS 6:19-20 What? Know ye not hat your body is the temple of the Holy Ghost which is in you, which ye have of God, and ye are not your own? For ye are bought with a price: therefore glorify God in your body, and in your spirit, which are God's. God created us and our bodies belong to Him. Every believer has the Holy Spirit living inside and they are basically a temple or a holy place. We should respect our bodies and take very good care of them so we can have a healthy life.

2 CORINTHIANS 3:18 But we all, with open face beholding as in a glass the glory of the Lord, are changed into the same image from glory to glory, even as by the Spirit of the Lord. In the old covenant, people were not allowed to see the glory of God. When Jesus died, the veil was torn and suddenly God was revealed as a living presence and not a piece of stone. Slowly, as we grow closer to God, our lives are becoming brighter and more beautiful.

2 CORINTHIANS 10:5 Casting down imaginations, and every high thing that exalteth itself against the knowledge of God, and bringing into captivity every thought to the obedience of Christ; We are told to take all our thoughts captive and make sure they are in line with what Christ asks of us. Many teachings and speculations today have no room for Christ and we need to make sure we compare them to the teachings of Jesus.

GALATIANS 6:2 Bear ye one another's burdens, and so fulfil the law of Christ. People struggle with many burdens today. This could include failures, temptations and trials. When we see someone struggling, we should come to help them in any possible way we can. Whatever we do for another human being, we are doing for God.

EPHESIANS 2:10 For we are his workmanship, created in Christ Jesus unto good works, which God hath before ordained that we should walk in them. A believer is a masterpiece of God. When we are saved through Jesus Christ, we are a new creation and we are to do good works. This doesn't mean we are saved <u>by</u> doing good works because we are saved by God's grace. This means we are saved <u>for</u> good works because when we follow Jesus we want to do good works. God has a blueprint for our life and it is our responsibility to discover His plan and obey His will. We can do this by staying connected to God, praying daily and reading scripture, confessing our sins, helping others in need and joining with other believers.

PHILIPPIANS 4:8 Finally, brethren, whatsoever things are true, whatsoever things are honest, whatsoever things are just, whatsoever things are pure, whatsoever things are lovely, whatsoever things are of good report; if there be any virtue, and if there be any praise, think on these things. The Bible teaches us that we are able to control our thoughts. We can't think negative thoughts and think about God at the same time. If an evil or negative thought comes into our head, we can immediately get rid of it through prayer and meditating on the Word of God. We should always keep our minds on things that are good and pure.

PHILIPPIANS 4:13 I can do all things through Christ which strengtheneth me. If something is in God's will, He will give us the strength to do it. It may be something difficult like overcoming a fear or doing something we didn't think we were capable of doing, but God will give us the necessary grace to accomplish the task.

1 TIMOTHY 4:8 For bodily exercise profiteth little: but godliness is profitable unto all things, having promise of the life that now is, and of that which is to come.
Exercise is important to keeping our bodies healthy while we are on this earth but its value is only temporary. Exercising unto our godliness is good for our body, soul and spirit and will be with us through eternity.

JAMES 2:1-4 My brethren, have not the faith of our Lord Jesus Christ, the Lord of glory, with respect of persons. For if there come unto your assembly a man with a gold ring, in goodly apparel, and there come in also a poor man in vile raiment; And ye have respect to him that weareth the gay clothing, and say unto him, Sit thou here in a good place; and say to the poor, Stand thou there, or sit here under my footstool: Are ye not then partial in yourselves, and are become judges of evil thoughts? There is no place in Christianity for favouritism or discrimination. We are supposed to respect everyone no matter who they are, where they come from or what kind of life they live. It doesn't matter if someone is dressed in rich clothing or poor clothing, we are all equal and we have no right to judge anyone else.

JAMES 3:2 For in many things we offend all. If any man offend not in word, the same is a perfect man, and able also to bridle the whole body. We have all said things that we wish we hadn't. Once a word is said, it can never be taken back and many times, great harm has already been done. If anyone is able to exercise self-control with words, then they should be able to control everything about themselves. Jesus was the only one who was able to accomplish this, but we should continue to try and follow his perfect example.

JAMES 4:14 Whereas ye know not what shall be on the morrow. For what is your life? It is even a vapour, that appeareth for a little time, and then vanisheth away.
We should be cautious about planning for tomorrow because we have no idea what will happen. Our human lives are temporary and could vanish at any time. We should focus on building our eternal life.

JAMES 4:15 For that ye ought to say, If the Lord will, we shall live, and do this, or that. We should consult God in all our plans. Our destiny is in His hands and we should live according to His wishes.

1 JOHN 3:1 Behold, what manner of love the Father hath bestowed upon us, that we should be called the sons of God: therefore the world knoweth us not, because it knew Him not. God has extended such marvelous love to us and we are called the children of God! Non-believers do not understand us because we have the same characteristics as Jesus and they don't understand Him either.